WAR ON WAR

BY THE SAME AUTHOR:

1. THE VIENNA DIVORCE. History of a dispute on the validity of conditional divorce in the 17th century. Lwow, 1931. (In Polish)
2. THE JEWISH EXCOMMUNICATION IN LITHUANIA IN THE 17th and 18th CENTURIES. Lwow, 1932. (In Polish)
3. THE RIGHT OF THE DISSOLUTION OF PARLIAMENT. Study on a problem of Constitutional Law. Lwow, 1933. (In Polish)
4. HISTORY OF THE BAR IN ANCIENT POLAND. Lwow, 1936. (In Polish)
5. THE PROTECTION OF JEWISH RELIGIOUS RIGHTS BY ROYAL EDICTS IN ANCIENT POLAND. New York, 1943. (In English)
6. THE DESTRUCTION OF EUROPE. New York, 1948. (In Yiddish)
7. AFTER THE DESTRUCTION. New York, 1950. (In Yiddish)
8. RELIGIOUS JEWRY AND THE UNITED NATIONS. Addresses before the United Nations. New York, 1953. (In English)
9. IN THE STRUGGLE AGAINST DISCRIMINATION. Addresses before various organs of the United Nations and of the Congress of the United States. New York, 1957. (In English)
10. LATE SUMMER FRUIT. Essays. New York, 1960. (In English)
11. THE JEWS IN OLD POLAND. Historical studies. Buenos Aires, 1962. (In Yiddish)
12. THESE WILL I REMEMBER. Biographies of leaders of religious Jewry in Europe who perished during the years 1939-1945. 6 volumes. New York, 1956-1965. (In Hebrew—editor).

WAR ON WAR

A proposal for effective international peacekeeping machinery based upon an account of the United Nations Security Council's attempts to deal with recent threats to world peace (The Far East, Middle East and Czechoslovakia.)

by

Dr. ISAAC LEWIN
Professor of History, Yeshiva University

SHENGOLD PUBLISHERS
NEW YORK, N. Y.

Library of Congress Catalog Card Number: 72-84914
Published by Shengold Publishers, Inc., New York
Copyright © 1969 by Dr. Isaac Lewin
All rights reserved
Printed in the United States of America

"The opinions of philosophers with regard to the conditions of the possibility of a public peace, shall be taken into consideration by states armed for war."

IMMANUEL KANT.

"Perpetual Peace,"
English translation
by M. Campbell Smith,
New York, 1903, p. 158.

CONTENTS

	page
Introduction	7
Chapter 1. The Korean War	11
Chapter 2. War in the Middle East 1956	30
Chapter 3. The War in Vietnam	56
Chapter 4. War in the Middle East 1967	78
Chapter 5. The Pueblo Incident	133
Chapter 6. The Czechoslovakian Crisis	144
Chapter 7. A Possible Solution	179

The quotations in Chapters 1-6 are from the Verbatim Records of the Security Council.

INTRODUCTION

THE TIME HAS come for the civilized world to declare war on war. The proposition sounds paradoxical, but its truth cannot be gainsaid. Only a world-wide concentrated effort can erase the greatest imaginable offense against humanity—the waging of war.

Murder is universally recognized as a crime. If one individual knowingly and intentionally kills another, he is arrested, tried, sentenced and put into jail. But when governments engage in mass murder, in the wanton destruction of thousands or even millions of lives, their efforts are legitimized and individual killings are glowingly characterized as acts of heroism. It is time to remove our blinders and recognize war for what it is—the greediest and bloodiest of vampires, a beast that is never sated.

War must be unconditionally and irrevocably outlawed. It must be stripped of every vestige of legitimacy, and since nations cannot be trusted to keep the peace out of self-interest, ways must be found to *enforce* peace.

The history of man's efforts to secure peace shows that humanity has never committed itself fully and unconditionally to the proposition that war *per se* is evil—that it cannot, under any circumstances, be resorted to as a means of settling international differences.

From the early fourteenth century, when Pierre Dubois wrote *De Recuperatione Terrae Sanctae,* until the momentous signing of the Charter of the United Nations at San Francisco on June 26, 1945, civilized society has vainly sought to

INTRODUCTION

insure world peace. The 1920 Covenant of the League of Nations was no more successful in this attempt than the *Defensor Pacis* by Marsilius of Padua and John of Jandun in 1324; the Kellogg-Briand Pact of 1928 was as futile as the 1461 peace proposal of George Podebrad of Bohemia and *The Complaint of Peace* of Erasmus in 1517. In short, we have not progressed materially in this century beyond the totally ineffective proposals of bygone days. Our contemporary machinery offers no greater hope of lasting world peace than the Utopian schemes of Emeric Crucé (author of *Le Nouveau Cynée*) who urged an international arbitration proposal in 1623, and of Maximilien Sully who, at about the same time, suggested a federation of states in his *Grand Design*.

The common thread that runs through this history of well-intentioned futility is reluctance to condemn war as intolerable and inadmissible under any and all conditions and to *enforce* peace.

Article 33 of the United Nations Charter—the furthest mankind has been prepared to go—urges member nations of the U.N. who are parties to any dispute "the continuance of which is likely to endanger the maintenance of international peace and security" to seek, *first of all*, "a solution by negotiation, enquiry, mediation, conciliation, arbitration, judicial settlement, resort to regional agencies or arrangements or other peaceful means of their choice." But such a mild exhortation is no more a deterrent to the use of force than were the provisions of the Hague Peace Conventions of 1899 and 1907. For no greater moral or practical discouragement to war is recognized by the United Nations Charter than its provision that "the Security Council shall, when it deems necessary, call upon the parties to settle their dispute by such [peaceful] means." Is there really no more effective method for insuring

WAR ON WAR

peace than to empower the Security Council to "call upon" potential combatants to desist? Is the framing of such a puny request all that the civilized world is prepared to do to prevent the methodical organized extinction of human lives?

The signatories to the United Nations Charter were not ignorant of the ravages of war. The preamble to the Charter notes explicitly that it is the purpose of the organization "to save succeeding generations from the scourge of war, which twice in our lifetime has brought untold sorrow to mankind." Indeed, the first purpose of the United Nations, specified in Article 1 of the Charter, is "to maintain international peace and security, and to that end: to take effective collective measures for the prevention and removal of threats to the peace, and for the suppression of acts of aggression or other breaches of the peace." The most patent "threat to the peace" is the possibility of war; the most obvious way to "suppress" aggression is to take clear-cut and unequivocal steps to eliminate that possibility or, when war has already begun, to *enforce* peace. Yet the historic constitution of the world's greatest and best hope for lasting peace—the Charter of the United Nations—does not outlaw war as a means of settling international differences. It pleads and cajoles where it should, by any reasonable standard, prohibit and condemn in no uncertain terms. It does not provide any machinery for enforcing peace on belligerent nations. The calculated destruction of millions of innocent human beings is as easy to perform in 1969 as it ever was before.

How can the moral principles upon which the United Nations was founded be reconciled with resort to war under any circumstances? Yet the Charter is silent on all but a sequence of priorities. Do not go to war, it says, unless you have exhausted all peaceful avenues. It is the "unless" clause which

INTRODUCTION

has, in one form or another, bedeviled and undermined every peace proposal for the past six centuries.

In recent years we have witnessed several tests of the effectiveness of the United Nations' peace-keeping machinery.

Several major wars have erupted since 1950, and each time the Security Council has made desperate efforts to bring about peace. But the wars in Korea, Vietnam and the Middle East have demonstrated unequivocally that the Security Council is, in effect, powerless to exert a meaningful influence in the maintenance of peace. An attempt made in January 1968 to submit the "Pueblo Incident" between the United States and North Korea to the Security Council for a decision did not progress beyond the stage of "consultations" among the Security Council members. The Czechoslovakian crisis in August 1968 was debated by the Security Council, but no solution was found.

The following chapters relate what was done by the Security Council in 1950-52 (Korea), 1956 (Middle East), 1966 (Vietnam), 1967 (Middle East), January 1968 (Pueblo Crisis) and August 1968 (Czechoslovakia). They will be followed by a concrete proposal for the establishment of more effective peace-keeping machinery within the framework of the United Nations.

Will such a proposal find a willing ear in the councils of the world? Will nations be prepared to commit themselves to firm and binding procedures designed to keep the world from the destruction wrought by savage bloodshed?

The answer is probably that voiced by the Prophet Ezekiel when, confronted by a valley filled with dry human bones, he was asked, "Son of man, can these bones live?"

- "O Lord, Thou knowest."

CHAPTER ONE

THE KOREAN WAR

ON JUNE 25, 1950, the North Korean army crossed the Thirty-eighth Parallel. In America, on the other side of the International Date Line, it was still June 24, a Saturday.

At 3 o'clock on the morning of Sunday, June 25, 1950 Trygve Lie, the Secretary-General of the United Nations, was awakened and was given the following telephone message from the United States Mission:

> "The United States Ambassador to the Republic of Korea has informed the Department of State that North Korean forces invaded the territory of the Republic of Korea at several points in the early morning hours of June 25 (Korean time). Pyongyang Radio, under the control of the North Korean regime, it is reported, has broadcast a declaration of war against the Republic of Korea effective 9 p.m. E.D.T. June 24. An attack of the forces of the North Korean regime under the circumstances referred to above constitutes a breach of the peace and an act of aggression. Upon the urgent request of my Government, I ask you to call an immediate meeting of the Security Council of the United Nations."

The Secretary-General informed the President of the Security Council of the request of the United States Government and a meeting was called for the same day at 2 p.m. Before the meeting was opened, a cable arrived from the United Nations Commission on Korea which read as follows:

THE KOREAN WAR

"Government of Republic of Korea states that about 04.00 hrs 25 June attacks were launched in strength by North Korean forces all along the 38th Parallel. Major points of attack have included Ongjin Peninsula, Kaesong area and Chunchon and east coast where seaborne landings have been reported north and south of Kangnung. Another seaborne landing reported imminent under air cover in Pohang area on southeast coast. The latest attacks have occurred along the parallel directly north of Seoul along shortest avenue of approach."

After reporting on the emergency session of the Korean Government, the cable went on to say that "the Commission wishes to draw attention of Secretary-General to serious situation developing which is assuming character of full-scale war and may endanger the maintenance of international peace and security."

At the meeting of the Security Council, at which the representative of the Soviet Union did not appear*, the two messages were put on the agenda. The representative of the Government of the Republic of Korea was invited to sit at the Council table during the consideration of the question. A discussion took place in which the representatives of the United States (Mr. Ernest A. Gross), United Kingdom (Sir Terence Shone), China (Mr. T. F. Tsiang), France (Mr. Chauvel), Cuba (Mr. C. Blanco), Ecuador (Mr. Correa) and Egypt (Mr. Mahmoud Favzi Bey) participated. The representative

---

* The Soviet Union walked out of the Security Council on January 10, 1950, after the President (Mr. T. F. Tsiang of China) had ruled that the USSR draft resolution (S/1443) to exclude the representative of the Chinese National Government from the Security Council be printed and distributed to members of the Council, and a special meeting be called for its consideration. Mr. Yakov Malik, the Soviet Ambassador challenged this ruling, which was sustained by 8 votes against 2 (USSR, Yugoslavia), with one abstention (India). Malik declared after the vote that he "cannot participate in the work of he Security Council or take part in this meeting of the Council until the Kuomintang representative has been excluded from membership in the Council." The Soviet Ambassador subsequently left the Council chamber. (Official Records of the 459 meeting of the Security Council, p. 4).

of Korea (Mr. Chang) was also heard. The U.S. representative presented a draft resolution calling upon the North Korean authorities to cease hostilities and to withdraw their armed forces to the border along the 38th Parallel; it requested the United Nations Commission on Korea to observe the withdrawal of the North Korean forces to the 38th Parallel and to keep the Security Council informed on the execution of the resolution; finally, it called "upon all Members to render every assistance to the United Nations in the execution of this resolution and to refrain from giving assistance to the North Korean authorities."

The representative of Yugoslavia (Mr. Nincic) felt that the messages and reports so far received were not sufficiently complete and balanced to enable the Council to fix final and definite responsibility. He therefore suggested that an opportunity should be granted to a representative of North Korea for a hearing. The resolution presented by Yugoslavia called for an immediate cessation of hostilities and for an invitation to the Government of North Korea to state its case.

The resolution presented by the United States was adopted by the Security Council by 9 votes with one abstention (Yugoslavia) and one member absent (Soviet Union).

Two days later, on June 27, 1950, the Security Council was convened again. Cables from the United Nations Commission on Korea were read at the beginning of the meeting. The Commission notified the Council that "having considered the latest reports of its military observers resulting from direct observation along the 38th Parallel during the period ending 48 hours before hostilities had begun, its present view was that the authorities in North Korea were carrying out a well-planned, concerted and full-scale invasion of South Korea,

THE KOREAN WAR

and that South Korean forces had been deployed on a wholly defensive basis on all sectors of the 38th Parallel."

Subsequently, Warren Austin, the representative of the United States, declared that although the Security Council's decision of June 25 had been made known to the North Korean authorities, they had "completely disregarded and flouted" that decision. It was, therefore, the plain duty of the Council to invoke stringent sanctions to restore internal peace." He read to the Council a statement made that day by the President of the United States of America, Harry S. Truman. The statement recalled that the Government forces in Korea, which were armed to prevent border raids and to preserve international security, had been attacked by invading North Korean forces that the invading troops had continued their hostilities despite the Security Council resolution of June 25; and that the Security Council had called upon all Members of the United Nations to render every assistance to the United Nations in the execution of that resolution. In these circumstances, the U.S. representative said, the President had ordered United States air and sea forces to give the Korean government troops cover and support.

The United States representative then submitted the following draft resolution:

> "*The Security Council,*
> *Having determined* that the armed attack upon the Republic of Korea by forces from North Korea constitutes a breach of peace;
> *Having called for* an immediate cessation of hostilities; and
> *Having called upon* the authorities of North Korea to withdraw forthwith their armed forces to the 38th Parallel; and

Having noted from the report of the United Nations Commission on Korea that the authorities in North Korea have neither ceased hostilities nor withdrawn their armed forces to the 38th Parallel and that urgent military measures are required to restore international peace and security; and

Having noted the appeal from the Republic of Korea to the United Nations for immediate and effective steps to secure peace and security,

Recommends that the Members of the United Nations furnish such assistance to the Republic of Korea as may be necessary to repel the armed attack and to restore international peace and security in the area."

The representative of Yugoslavia (Mr. Bebler) opposed the American resolution. He maintained that "the Security Council could not and should not, after only two days of fighting, abandon all hope that the parties involved would at last understand the interests of their own people and of international peace; the Council could not be certain that they would continue to refuse, at that fateful hour, to enter into negotiations." He submitted his own draft resolution stating that the Security Council "decides to renew its call for the cessation of hostilities and draw the attention of the parties involved to the grave consequences which a prolongation of operations would entail, both for the people of Korea and for international peace and security." The second point in the Yugoslav draft resolution called for a decision by the Security Council "to initiate a procedure of mediation between the two parties involved in armed conflict, and call upon the said parties to accept such procedure in principle." Finally, it suggested that the Government of the People's Democratic Republic of Korea; i.e., North Korea as distinct from South Korea, be invited at once to send a representative to the Headquarters of

THE KOREAN WAR

the United Nations with full powers to participate in the procedure of mediation.

The United States draft resolution was adopted by seven votes to one (Yugoslavia) with one member absent (USSR) and two members (Egypt, India) not voting because complete instructions from their governments had not yet been obtained. Egypt later declared that it would have abstained; India joined the majority in accepting the American resolution.

The Secretary-General immediately transmitted the text of the adopted Security Council resolution to all members of the United Nations, whereupon Andrei Gromyko, Deputy Minister for Foreign Affairs of the Union of Soviet Socialist Republics, sent the following cable to the Secretary-General:

"The Soviet Union Government has received from you the text of the Security Council resolution of 27 June 1950 calling the attention of Members of the United Nations to the necessity of intervening in Korean affairs in the interest of the South Korean authorities. The Soviet Union Government notes that this resolution was adopted by six votes, the seventh vote being that of the Kuomintang representative, Mr. Tingfu F. Tsiang, who has no legal right to represent China, whereas the United Nations Charter requires that a Security Council resolution must be adopted by seven votes including those of the five permanent members of the Council; namely the United States, the United Kingdom, France, the Union of Soviet Socialist Republics and China. As is known, moreover, the above resolution was passed in the absence of two permanent members of the Security Council, the Union of Soviet Socialist Republics and China, whereas under the United Nations Charter a decision of the Security Council on an important matter can only be made with the concurring votes of all five permanent members of the Council; viz. the United States, the United Kingdom, France, the Union of Soviet Socialist Republics and China. In view of the foregoing it is quite clear that the said resolution of the Security Council on the Korean question has no legal force."

Nevertheless, the Security Council went ahead with the promised support to the Republic of Korea. On July 7, 1950, the representative of the United Kingdom suggested at a meeting of the Security Council that the assistance which the resolution of June 27 had recommended for the cause of the Republic of Korea, be co-ordinated. He submitted a joint French-United Kingdom draft resolution which read as follows:

> "*The Security Council,*
> *Having determined* that the armed attack upon the Republic of Korea by forces from North Korea constitutes a breach of peace,
> *Having recommended* that Members of the United Nations furnish such assistance to the Republic of Korea as may be necessary to repel the armed attack and to restore international peace and security in the area,
> 1. *Welcomes* the prompt and vigorous support which governments and peoples of the United Nations have given to its resolutions of 25 and 27 June 1950 to assist the Republic of Korea in defending itself against armed attack and thus to restore international peace and security in the area;
> 2. *Notes* that Members of the United Nations have transmitted to the United Nations offers of assistance for the Republic of Korea;
> 3. *Recommends* that all Members providing military forces and other assistance pursuant to the aforesaid Security Coun-

THE KOREAN WAR

cil resolutions make such forces and other assistance available to a unified command under the United States;

4. *Requests* the United States to designate the commander of such forces;

5. *Authorizes* the unified command at its discretion to use the United Nations flag in the course of operations against North Korean forces concurrently with the flags of the various nations participating;

6. *Requests* the United States to provide the Security Council with reports as appropriate on the course of action taken under the unified command."

This resolution was adopted by a 7 to 0 vote, with 3 abstentions (Egypt, India, Yugoslavia). Once again, the Soviet Union was absent and did not vote, its official position remaining the same as it had expressed with regard to the resolution of June 25 and 27. By a letter of July 13, 1950, the Soviet representative transmitted to the Secretary-General the text of a statement made by Mr. Gromyko on the Korean question. The statement said that "the events in Korea had broken out as a result of a provocative attack by the troops of the South Korean authorities on the frontier areas of the Korean People's Democratic Republic and that the attack had been the outcome of a premeditated plan."

Mr. Gromyko added in his statement that "when during the very first days of the conflict it became clear that the terrorist regime of Syngman Rhee, which had never enjoyed the support of the Korean people, was collapsing, the United States had resorted to open intervention in Korea, ordering its air, naval and subsequently its ground forces, to take action on the side of the South Korean authorities against the Korean people. Thereby the United States Government had gone over from a policy of preparing aggression to outright acts of aggression, and had embarked on a course of open intervention in Korea's domestic affairs, on a course of armed intervention in Korea. Having taken that course, the United States Government violated peace, demonstrating thereby that, far from seeking to consolidate peace, it is on the contrary an enemy of peace."

Mr. Gromyko's statement was made on July 4, three days before the July 7 meeting of the Security Council. It attacked both the United States Government and the Security Council. "The illegal resolution of 27 June," said the Soviet Deputy Minister of Foreign Affairs, "adopted by the Security Council under pressure from the United States Government, showed that the Security Council was acting not as a body charged with the main responsibility for the maintenance of peace, but as a tool utilized by ruling circles of the United States for the unleashing of war. That resolution constituted a hostile act against peace. If the Security Council had valued the cause of peace, it should have attempted to reconcile the fighting sides in Korea before it had adopted such a scandalous resolution. Neither the Security Council nor the Secretary-General had made such an attempt. On the contrary, the Secretary-General, far from fulfilling his direct duties to observe the exact fulfilment of the United Nations Charter, had obsequiously helped a gross violation of the Charter, along with the United States Government and other members of the Security Council."

If such was the reaction of the Government of the Soviet Union to the resolution of the Security Council of June 27, one could expect even greater indignation as a result of the subsequent adoption of the France-United Kingdom proposal on July 7. On July 11, Mr. Gromyko cabled to the Secretary-General that "the Soviet Union Government finds that the

THE KOREAN WAR

adoption of this resolution constitutes the same flagrant violation of the United Nations Charter as the Security Council of 27 June on the Korean question." The cable finished by declaring "that the Security Council resolution of 7 July, first, is illegal, and secondly, constitutes a direct act of assistance to armed aggression against the Korean people."

* * *

A full-scale war developed, in which more than 1,000,000 men fought on behalf of North Korea. From the Manchurian fields near the Yalu river 2,000 planes supported the North Korean army. Pitted against them were seven divisions of the United States Army. Additional troops were supplied by fifteen other members of the United Nations. Five other member nations sent medical assistance, and forty-six contributed economic assistance. South Korean military forces totalled 400,000 men.

* * *

The USSR returned to the Security Council after an absence of six months when its turn came to assume the presidency of the Council. On August 1, 1950, the first meeting was held with the representative of the USSR (Mr. Malik) in the chair. At the beginning of the meeting he ruled "that the representative of the Kuomintang group seated in the Security Council did not represent China and therefore could not take part in the Council's meetings." That ruling was immediately challenged by the representatives of the United States (Mr. Austin), United Kingdom (Sir Gladwyn Jebb), and France (Mr. Chauvel). The proposal to overrule the President's ruling was adopted by 8 votes to 3 (India, USSR, Yugoslavia), whereupon the representative of the United States moved to consider, as the meeting's next item, the "Complaint of aggression upon the Republic of Korea." The representative of the USSR, who presided, had previously put on the provisional agenda, as the next item, the "Peaceful settlement of the Korean question."

It took the Security Council two days to reach a decision on what to call the subject on the agenda. The motion of the United States representative on this matter was adopted by 8 votes to 1 (USSR), with 2 abstentions (India, Yugoslavia).

A lengthy discussion ensued on the problem of the participation of both Koreas in the deliberations of the Council. Sir Gladwyn Jebb, the representative of the United Kingdom, expressed the opinion that the representation, at the Council table, of the Republic of Korea on the one hand, and of the North Korean authorities on the other hand, were "two separate questions." He added that the Council already had previously decided to invite the representative of the Republic of Korea to take his place at the table and there could be no suggestion that he should not be invited. When it came to the second question, the situation was that the North Korean authorities had, by their refusal to obey the injunctions of the United Nations, "put themselves in a state of hostility with the United Nations itself." These authorities should certainly not be excluded forever, but "they must first by their behavior put themselves right with the United Nations."

The representative of the USSR, who presided, explained that "his delegation's proposal was based upon the actual state of affairs in Korea, which was that there were two government camps, one in North Korea and the other in South Korea. The Korean people, which was one and the same both in the north and in the south, was divided into two opposing factions by an internal struggle and civil war. If the Council,

THE KOREAN WAR

setting aside all secondary circumstances, approached the factual situation realistically and invited the representatives of both sides, it would, in his view, be taking the most objective and the fairest decision possible."

In the discussion, Warren Austin, the representative of the United States, posed a series of questions and answers in the following terms:

> Whose troops are attacking deep in somebody else's territory? Those of the North Koreans. Whose territory is overrun by an invading army? That of the Republic of Korea. Who is assisting the Republic of Korea to defend itself? The United Nations, with the support of fifty-three of the fifty-nine Members. Who has the influence and the power to call off the invading North Korean army? The Soviet Union. Who is responsible for the bombing and bloodshed that inevitably ensued from the act of aggression? The North Koreans and those who support them. Who, then, can stop the bombing and the bloodshed? The North Koreans and those who support their aggression. What member of the Security Council is supporting the North Korean regime in the Security Council? The Soviet Union. What kind of a 'peaceful settlement' has the Soviet Union proposed? The kind of settlement that would send the United Nations police away and leave the bandits to plunder Korea at will. Who, then, is supporting the United Nations Charter and really working for peace? The fifty-three Members of the United Nations which are supporting the Republic of Korea. Is the USSR one of the fifty-three? No."

The Security Council found itself in a procedural quagmire. Various representatives asked for a ruling by the President, but the latter refused to rule. Some challenged his attitude, calling it a ruling. He responded that since there was no ruling, nothing could be challenged. According to the official report of the Security Council to the General Assembly, "he declared that he had not given, was not giving, and was not in a position to give a ruling on the point in question."

The reports of the United Nations Commission on Korea were cited by some representatives as proof that North Korea was the aggressor. The Soviet representative, who presided, declared these reports to be worthless because the information contained in them had been received "from the United States and Syngman Rhee sources." Citing statements by the Soviet Government and by the Soviet delegation in the Council, he said that "numerous facts had been adduced to show that the events in Korea had taken place as the result of a provocative attack by the forces of the South Korean authorities on areas of the People's Democratic Republic of Korea lying to the north of the 38th Parallel."

On August 14, 1950, at a meeting of the Security Council, the representative of Ecuador (Mr. Quevedo) pointed out that since August 1, "the Council remained paralysed and thus had weakened the hope of the peoples of the world for peace." He felt that "the world would not accept the version that the invaded Republic of Korea was the aggressor, or that the United Nations Commission on Korea, composed of representatives of sovereign States, could be a mere tool of the United States." The representative of France (Mr. Chauvel) welcomed the return of the Soviet representative and noted that "since the latter had taken over the Presidency, the Council had not been able even to begin discussing the agenda." He expressed the view that "the USSR delegation, which had been absent on 25 June, had by its systematic failure to appear failed in its obligations." The presiding Soviet representative immediately replied that "the Charter did not require from

THE KOREAN WAR

each member of the Council obligatory participation in its meetings in all circumstances."

During the month of August, 1950, the discussion between the Soviet representative and the other members of the Security Council continued without any vote being taken. Debate occasionally became quite heated. On August 22, the Soviet representative accused the United States of being the real aggressor. "The whole world knew," he said, "that armed intervention in the internal affairs of the Korean people, armed aggression in Korea, was being carried out by United States forces on the personal orders of President Truman and under the command of a United States general. No illegal resolutions could veil or justify that aggression." He further said that "for the purpose of concealing that colonial brigandage, the United States Government, with the support of the governments of other colonial Powers, was exerting every effort to compel certain colonial slaves and 'Marshallized' lackeys to send a certain number of their troops to Korea in order to give United States military operations in Korea and the Far East an appearance of being international." The representatives of the United Kingdom and the United States answered with growing impatience. Sir Gladwyn Jebb recalled "Stalin's statement, in November 1939, that it was not Germany who attacked France and Britain, but France and Britain who attacked Germany." Ambassador Austin said that "the representative of the USSR used propaganda devices to cover the truth, calling falsehoods irrefutable facts."

For the month of September the Presidency of the Security Council went to the representative of the United Kingdom who invited the Republic of Korea to take a seat at the Council table. His decision was upheld by the Security Council. On

WAR ON WAR

September 6, 1950, a United States draft resolution, reading as follows, was put to a vote:

> "*The Security Council*
> *Condemns* the North Korean authorities for their continued defiance of the United Nations;
> *Calls upon* all States to use their influence to prevail upon the authorities of North Korea to cease this defiance;
> *Calls upon* all States to refrain from assisting or encouraging the North Korean authorities and to refrain from action which might lead to the spread of the Korean conflict to other areas and thereby further endanger international peace and security."

There were 9 votes in favor, one against (USSR), and one abstention (Yugoslavia). Since the negative vote was cast by a permanent member of the Council, the draft resolution was not adopted.

At the same meeting, a Soviet draft resolution (originally introduced on August 4) was also put to a vote. It read:

> "*The Security Council*
> *Decides*
> (a) To consider it necessary, in the course of the discussion of the Korean question, to invite the representative of the People's Republic of China and also to hear representatives of the Korean people;
> (b) To put an end to the hostilities in Korea and at the same time to withdraw foreign troops from Korea."

This resolution was rejected by 8 votes to 1 (USSR) with 2 abstentions (Egypt, Yugoslavia).

Another Soviet draft resolution calling upon "the Government of the United States of America to cease and not

THE KOREAN WAR

permit in future the bombing by the Air Force or by other means of towns and populated areas and also the shooting up from the air of the peaceful population of Korea," was debated at the Security Council meeting held on September 7. The Soviet representative charged that the armed forces of the United States had perpetrated numerous atrocities in Korea. He alleged that this constituted a gross violation of universally recognized standards of international law, particularly of Article 25 of the Fourth Hague Convention and Article 1 of the Ninth Hague Convention. "The brutal and inhuman mass bombing of Korean towns and villages," said the Soviet representative, "and the rocket shelling and machine-gunning by American air and naval forces, of the civilian population in Korean towns, villages and fields, were resulting in the total destruction of many towns and populated centres and the brutal slaughter of many thousands of non-combatants, including women, children and old people, who had already fallen victims to the terroristic and barbarous actions of the United States armed forces in Korea." The representative of the United States answered that the air activity of the United Nations forces in Korea had been and was directed solely at military targets of the invader, but that the Communist command had compelled civilians to work on these sites, had used peaceful villages to cover its tanks and civilian dress to disguise its soldiers. Alleged violations of the Hague Conventions should be investigated by the International Red Cross, the U.S. representative said, but he added that representatives of that organization had not been allowed into areas under the control of North Korean forces.

The Security Council rejected the USSR draft resolution by 9 votes to one (USSR), with one abstention (Yugoslavia). The representative of the USSR stated that he considered it illegal and unjust that the majority in the Council had rejected the draft resolution.

At the ensuing meeting of the Security Council new charges were exchanged between the USSR and the United States. On September 18, the representative of the United States, Warren Austin, read a report of the United Nations Command Operations in Korea, according to which "positive proof had been obtained that, during 1949 and 1950, the Soviet Union had supplied the North Korean Forces with munitions and that the Chinese Communists had supplied manpower." Ambassador Malik answered that the U.S. representative's assertion was slanderous and in no way conformed to the facts. He repeated his statement made previously on August 11:

> "The representative of the United States is not the only one to make such slanderous statements. That famous warmonger, Mr. Churchill, and some of his followers are also spreading similar slander by asserting that the Soviet Union is providing North Korea with jet-propelled aircraft. These inventions of Mr. Churchill's do not correspond to the facts, but are fabrications from beginning to end."

Malik further said that "even the press in the United States had admitted that Syngman Rhee and the United States troops in Korea had already lost almost as much fighting equipment as had been lost by the United States during the entire European campaign. It was not surprising that the Korean army was well equipped, as it had been able to equip itself from captured booty." A new draft resolution was subsequently introduced by the Soviet representative to the effect that the Security Council called upon the Government of the

THE KOREAN WAR

United States "to cease, and henceforth forbid, the bombardment by air forces or by other means of peaceful towns and inhabited centres and also the machine-gunning from the air of the peaceful population of Korea."

The representative of the United States commented on the new draft resolution at a meeting held on September 30, 1950. "The purpose of the charges levelled by the USSR delegation against the United Nations forces in Korea," he said, "was at least twofold: first, to appeal to the natural abhorrence which all men felt for war and, in particular, for the tragic aspects of bombing; secondly, it constituted an attempt to single out the United States as a special offender in order to divert attention from the fact that it was the United Nations which was engaged in the action in Korea."

The new draft resolution of the USSR was again rejected by 9 votes to 1 (USSR), with one abstention (Yugoslavia).

* * *

The official records of the Security Council beginning with October 1950 show a constantly increasing tension. The representatives of the Soviet Union and the United States were engaged in an exchange which was, in effect, verbal warfare.

On one occasion, the Soviet representative said that "it was known that the United States delegation and the delegations of other countries bound by a military alliance—the aggressive North Atlantic Treaty—long ago had begun to violate the fundamental provisions of the Charter, and that they were always trying to make slanderous accusations against other countries, without listening to their representatives. In order to form a definite opinion on any case, it was necessary to hear both sides. Obviously, it was much more pleasant for United States representatives to lounge at meetings and hurl

WAR ON WAR

indiscriminate accusations right and left without bothering to hear the opinion of those whom they were accusing."

The atmosphere in the Security Council was not conducive to peace. After fierce fighting over a full year, Yakov Malik, the representative of the USSR to the Security Council, proposed in a radio address, delivered on June 23, 1951, that "discussions should be started between the belligerents for a cease-fire and an armistice providing for the mutual withdrawal of forces from the 38th Parallel."

On July 8, 1951, representatives of the two fighting armies met in Kaesong. More than two years passed before the fighting finally ceased.

On July 30, 1951, it was agreed in Kaesong that hostilities should continue while negotiations were in progress. At that time 750,000 Chinese and North Koreans confronted 500,000 United Nations troops. Both armies suffered heavy losses; some military operations (like that of Heartbreak Ridge, October 1951) caused tens of thousands of casualties. Fighting never stopped during the armistice negotiations.

When the cease-fire was finally signed at Panmunjom, on July 27, 1953, and the fighting ended, both armies began to count the casualties. It took years until the count was final. Today we know it.

Total United States casualties: 144,173.

Total South Korean casualties: 1,312,836.

Total Chinese and North Korean casualties: 1,540,000.

This is the net result of the Security Council's failure to stop war in June, 1950.

CHAPTER TWO

WAR IN THE MIDDLE EAST 1956

ON JULY 26, 1956, the Government of Egypt nationalized the Suez Canal Company, thereby abruptly terminating the Suez Canal Convention of 1888. To be sure, the law under which the Suez Canal Company was nationalized did provide for compensation to the shareholders and set up a new Canal authority independent of governmental regulations. However, the governments of France and the United Kingdom viewed this new situation as constituting a grave danger to free and open shipping through the Canal. Consequently, they called a conference in London for August 16, at which eighteen States adopted proposals for the operation of the Canal. Egypt refused to participate in the conference or to negotiate on the basis of these proposals. The tension created by the action of July 26 mounted.

On September 12, 1956, the French and British representatives to the United Nations wrote a letter to the President of the Security Council, informing him of "the aggravation of the situation which, if allowed to continue, would constitute a manifest danger to peace and security." The representative of Egypt responded on September 17 by stating that the French and British claim was "completely devoid of any legal, historical and moral foundation."

WAR ON WAR

The next step taken was an official request by France and the United Kingdom, on September 23, 1956, for a meeting of the Security Council to consider "the situation created by the unilateral action of the Egyptian Government in bringing to an end the system of international operation of the Suez Canal, which was confirmed and completed by the Suez Canal Convention of 1888." Egypt also requested a meeting of the Council to consider "actions against Egypt by some powers, particularly France and the United Kingdom, which constitute a danger to international peace and security and serious violations of the Charter of the United Nations."

The Council met on September 26, 1956. The item proposed by France and the United Kingdom was unanimously included on the agenda. The item proposed by Egypt was also included, but there the vote was 7 to 0, with four abstentions (Australia, Belgium, France and the United Kingdom).

The discussion of the item proposed by France and the United Kingdom began on October 5. The two powers submitted a joint draft resolution endorsing the proposals of the eighteen States. British Foreign Secretary Selwyn Lloyd, speaking first, gave the historical background of the Suez Canal concessions; he characterized the act of July 26, 1956, as a *coup d'état*. His government, he said, was determined to uphold its rights to free transport through the Suez Canal. His statement was supplemented by that of his French colleague, Pineau (President of the Security Council for that month) who said that "it was incumbent upon the United Nations to recognize that there could be no genuine peace without the maintenance of justice and international law, and to act firmly to restore international confidence."

The Soviet representative, Mr. Shepilov, speaking on October 8, stated that the nationalization of the Suez Canal

THE WAR IN THE MIDDLE EAST 1956

Company was exclusively Egypt's internal affair. The fact that the United Kingdom and France were applying military measures and economic sanctions against Egypt created a most serious situation in the Middle East. It was a policy of "sabre-rattling," constituted a grave violation of the basic principles of the United Nations Charter "and was particularly inadmissible on the part of permanent members of the Security Council." The appeal to the United Nations by France and the United Kingdom "was a procedure and not a policy." He immediately explained the meaning of these words:

> "What does this mean? It means, apparently, that the ruling circles in the United Kingdom and France intend to give the following reply to the imperious public demands for a peaceful settlement of the Suez problem: 'You have urged us to appeal to the United Nations. We have done so. We have appealed to the Security Council. But, as you see, it is powerless, it can do nothing. Negotiations with Egypt are useless. Other steps must be taken. Egypt is guilty. Crucify it!' "

Obviously, Mr. Shepilov anticipated the failure of the Security Council to solve the problem. He warned that "this approach is fraught with the gravest consequences; it is playing with fire."

It was indeed so. After protracted discussion at several public and private meetings, the Security Council voted on a draft resolution submitted by France and the United Kingdom. The resolution contained some principles for the future settlement of the Suez question (that there should be free and open transit through the Canal without discrimination; that the sovereignty of Egypt should be respected; that the operation of the Canal should be insulated from the politics of any country; that the manner of fixing tolls and charges should be decided by agreement between Egypt and the users; that a fair proportion of the dues should be allotted to development; that in case of disputes, they should be settled by arbitration). These principles, not being controversial, were adopted unanimously. The second part of the draft resolution, however, received nine votes for acceptance and two for rejection, and since one of the two votes against this part was that of the Soviet Union, a permanent member of the Security Council, it was not adopted.

The American representative, Secretary of State John Foster Dulles, expressed "regret that it has not been possible for the Council to agree on more than the principles, the requirements, of a settlement." However, he said, "that already is much." The President thanked the representatives present "for the spirit of understanding and courtesy they have shown during these discussions." He felt "justified in saying that this series of meetings of the Security Council has done great credit to the United Nations."

But this praise for the Security Council was premature. The unanimous decision concerning the principles of a future settlement was taken on October 13, 1956. Two weeks and two days later, war broke out.

* * *

Letter dated 29 October 1956 from the Representative of the United States of America addressed to the President of the Security Council. (S/3706)

"The Government of the United States has received information to the effect that in violation of the Armistice Agreement between Israel and Egypt, the armed forces of Israel have penetrated deeply into Egyptian territory. This military action

THE WAR IN THE MIDDLE EAST 1956

commenced October 29 and is continuing in the Sinai area. The situation makes imperative an immediate meeting of the Security Council, charged as it is with the primary responsibility for the maintenance of international peace and security as well as responsibility for the observance of the Armistice Agreement.

I have the honour, therefore, in behalf of my Government to request you to convene a meeting of the Security Council as soon as possible to consider 'The Palestine Question: Steps for the Immediate Cessation of the Military Action of Israel in Egypt.'

Accept, Excellency, etc.

(*Signed*) Henry Cabot Lodge, Jr.
Permanent Representative of the
United States of America."

* * *

The meeting opened on October 30, 1956, at 11 a.m.

The President, Mr. Bernard Cornut-Gentille of France, in opening the meeting, apologized to the members of the Council for inconveniencing them throughout the night while conveying to them the information concerning the outbreak of hostilities in the Middle East. After the adoption of the agenda—the letter of the United States representative of October 29—Ambassador Lodge, the United States representative, stated that "as the result of Israel's invasion of the Sinai Peninsula" the critical developments are "unfortunately still continuing." He said further that "failure by the Council to react at this time would be a clear avoidance of its responsibility for the maintenance of international peace and security."

His government, Mr. Lodge said, felt that it was "imperative that the Council act in the promptest manner to deter-

WAR ON WAR

mine that a breach of the peace has occurred, to order that the military action undertaken by Israel cease immediately, and to make clear its view that the Israel armed forces should be immediately withdrawn behind the established armistice lines." Nothing less would suffice, the Ambassador added, and he concluded his statement by saying:

> "We, as members of the Council, accordingly should call upon all Members of the United Nations to render prompt assistance in achieving a withdrawal of Israel forces. All Members, specifically, should refrain from giving any assistance which might continue or prolong the hostilities. No one, certainly, should take advantage of this situation for any selfish interest. Each of us here, and every Member of the United Nations, has a clear-cut responsibility to see that peace and stability of the Palestine area is restored forthwith. Anything less is an invitation to disaster in that part of the world. This is an immediate responsibility which derives from the Council's obligations under its cease-fire orders and the armistice agreements between the Israelis and the Arab States endorsed by this Security Council. It derives also, of course, from the larger responsibility under the United Nations Charter."

The Secretary-General of the United Nations, Dag Hammerskjold, reported orally on the information received by him from the Chief of Staff of the U.N. Truce Supervision Organization. He said that on October 30, 1956, at 02.17 local time, the Chief of Staff had transmitted to Israel's Minister for Foreign Affairs a communication requesting the withdrawal of troops and a cease-fire. A message had also been sent by the Chief of Staff to the Foreign Minister of Egypt informing him of the request made to Israel to withdraw its troops and asking concurrence by Egypt to a cease-fire to take effect at 12.00

THE WAR IN THE MIDDLE EAST 1956

local time, October 30, 1956. The Secretary-General had no information, so far, concerning replies, if any, by the Governments of Israel and Egypt.

Various representatives congratulated and thanked the United States delegation for the initiative it had taken. The Soviet Union's representative, Arkady Sobolev, had the following accusation to make:

> "It is plain from everything that is happening that Israel could not have made this attack without encouragement and help from those aggressive circles which are not interested in the preservation of peace in the Middle East and are trying to find some pretext for moving their troops into this area."

He quoted from a press report to the effect that the United Kingdom and France had declared that their forces would occupy key positions in the Suez Canal area unless Israel and Egypt stopped fighting within twelve hours. It was quite clear, said the Soviet Ambassador, that the intention was to intervene in the events in the Middle East "without waiting for United Nations action."

After reciprocal accusations by the representatives of Egypt and Israel, the meeting was adjourned until the afternoon.

In the afternoon, Sir Pierson Dixon, the United Kingdom representative, informed the Security Council of further developments in the crisis. His Prime Minister had made a statement in the House of Commons (after consultation with the French Prime Minister and Foreign Minister who had come over to London) in which he indicated that "unless hostilities can quickly be stopped, free passage through the Canal will be jeopardized." He then said:

WAR ON WAR

". . . as a result of the consultations held in London today, the United Kingdom and French Governments have now addressed urgent communications to the Governments of Egypt and Israel. In these we have called upon both sides to stop all warlike action by land, sea and air forthwith and to withdraw their military forces to a distance of ten miles from the Canal. Further, in order to separate the belligerents and to guarantee freedom of transit through the Canal by the ships of all nations, we have asked the Egyptian Government to agree that Anglo-French forces should move temporarily—I repeat, temporarily—into key positions at Port Said, Ismailia and Suez. The Governments of Egypt and Israel have been asked to answer this communication within twelve hours. It has been made clear to them that if, at the expiration of that time, one or both have not undertaken to comply with these requirements, British and French forces will intervene in whatever strength may be necessary to secure compliance."

After reading the text of the British Prime Minister's statement, which was also distributed in writing (S/3711), Sir Pierson Dixon read to the Council the communication which was handed to the *chargé d'affaires* of Israel in London at 4:15 p.m., and to the Egyptian Ambassador in London ten minutes later. Both communications were identical but, in order to complete the record, Sir Pierson read them twice. He added that "both sides (*i.e.* Egypt and Israel), in different ways, have shown such repeated disregard for the resolutions of the Security Council that we have felt confidence that we should have the general support of the Council, and the United Nations as a whole, for what we are doing—namely, everything in our power to bring about the earliest cessation of hostilities and to safeguard the free passage of the Canal."

THE WAR IN THE MIDDLE EAST 1956

Sir Pierson asked bluntly:

"How can we have confidence, much as we should like to, that some future injunction by the Security Council would in fact prove effective to deal, in time—and time is of the essence—with a situation which is rapidly getting out of control?"

He then complained about the ineffectiveness of the Charter:

"I need hardly remind the Council that unfortunately those provisions of the Charter which provided that the Council should have a military arm have never been put into effect. I need not go into the reasons why. The roadblocks have been placed by a permanent member of the Security Council, whose misuse of the veto has done much to complicate the situation in the Middle East and to bring us to the extremely grave situation which we now face."

He did not mean to say, Sir Pierson further stated, that "there is nothing that the Security Council can do in this situation." He believed that a correct judgment on the situation, which he was confident the Council would reach, could "materially aid the cause of peace." He ended his remarks, however, by expressing the opinion that "there is no action that the Security Council can constructively take which would contribute to the twin objectives of stopping the fighting and safeguarding free passage through the Suez Canal."

While the representative of France formally agreed with the British Ambassador's statements, the other members of the Security Council were not convinced.

The representative of the United States introduced a draft resolution calling upon Israel immediately to withdraw its armed forces behind the established armistice lines. It also called upon all members: "(a) to refrain from the use of force or threat of force in the area in any manner inconsistent with the purposes of the United Nations; (b) to assist the United Nations in ensuring the integrity of the armistice agreements; and (c) to refrain from giving any military, economic or financial assistance to Israel as long as it has not complied with this resolution." Ambassador Lodge expressed the belief that if this draft resolution were adopted and if Israel were to comply with it, the basis for the twelve-hour ultimatum which the United Kingdom and France had given to Egypt and Israel would disappear. He made it clear that he did not imply that under any circumstances would this ultimatum be justified or be found consistent with the purposes and principles of the United Nations Charter.

The American draft resolution was supported by the Soviet Union. Ambassador Sobolev stated that his delegation would vote for it and would submit no amendments.

After Israel and Egypt had been heard, the Council renewed the discussion. Some representatives felt that a vote on the American draft resolution was a matter of urgency (although others would have preferred a postponement in order to be able to receive instructions from their governments) because the ultimatum was to expire soon. The vote was taken. Seven members (China, Cuba, Iran, Peru, USSR, United States, Yugoslavia) were for the draft resolution; two (France, United Kingdom) against, and two (Australia, Belgium) abstained. Because the negative votes were from permanent members of the Council, the resolution failed of adoption.

In the impasse that was created, the Soviet representative took the initiative to propose that the Council adopt only part of the American draft resolution: (a) the preamble, and (b)

THE WAR IN THE MIDDLE EAST 1956

the call upon Israel to withdraw its armed forces behind the established armistice lines. The Chinese representative amended it to include also a call upon Israel and Egypt to cease fire immediately, which was accepted by the Soviet representative. The French and British representatives found this new draft resolution as "introducing a new element" or "an interesting one." They asked only for "an hour or an hour and a quarter" delay. The Soviet representative asked whether the two representatives could assure the Security Council that the ultimatum would not be put into effect until the Council had reached a decision on this question. No such assurance having been given, he considered that the proposal only indicated a continuation of the previous dilatory tactics.

A vote was then taken on the French motion in favor of adjournment until 9 p.m. The motion was adopted by 8 votes against 1 (USSR), with two abstentions (United States, Yugoslavia).

The permanent representative of Egypt had, during the meeting, addressed a letter to the President of the Council asking him for an immediate meeting of the Council "to consider the British-French act of aggression." The representative of Iran, supported by Yugoslavia, asked that the Egyptian letter be included in the provisional agenda for the evening session. The President and the Council agreed.

At the beginning of the evening session on October 30, 1956, the third in one day, Sir Pierson Dixon of the United Kingdom made a statement to the effect that he had by no means accepted the implications and statements contained in the letter from the representative of Egypt. The President of the Council (as representative of France) agreed wholeheartedly with the British representative. The provisional agenda was adopted, including both items (the letter from the U.S. representative as well as the Egyptian letter).

After a brief discussion as to whether the draft resolution should call "upon Israel and Egypt immediately to cease fire" or "upon all the parties concerned," the vote was taken on the draft resolution calling "upon Israel and Egypt immediately to cease fire." There were 7 votes in favor (Australia, China, Cuba, Iran, Peru, USSR, Yugoslavia), 2 against (France, United Kingdom), and 2 abstentions (Belgium, United States). Since the negative votes were from permanent members of the Council, the resolution was not adopted.

The Soviet representative commented that "the adjournment produced no favorable results, but the dilatory tactics resorted to in the Security Council had again won the day." Sir Pierson Dixon answered him that there was no question of filibustering. "Mr. Sobolev seems to have that term on the brain," said the British delegate. "I would observe that even the Security Council has a stomach, and I have in fact been in touch with my Government despite the difference of hour, and I have actually been acting on its instructions."

Mr. Sobolev then turned on the Security Council:

> "This has been a black day for the Security Council. Confronted with an act of aggression perpetrated against a Member State of the United Nations, the Security Council has shown itself to be incapable of action. A heavy burden of responsibility is thus placed on those members of the Council which prevented it from acting."

Concerning the essence of the problem he said:

> "It is now abundantly clear that Israel's invasion of Egypt was planned to provide a pretext for joint action by the

THE WAR IN THE MIDDLE EAST 1956

United Kingdom and France to seize the Suez Canal by force of arms."

And he repeated:

"I should like to place it on record that the Security Council's inability to take action prescribed by the Charter, its inability to take any measures at all, let alone effective measures, to deal with an act of aggression, places a heavy responsibility upon those members of the Council which prevented it from doing so."

The Security Council then discussed the Egyptian letter, the next item on the agenda. The representative of Egypt, Omar Loutfi, again expressed the hope, "echoing the words of the United States representative," that no State which was a Member of the United Nations would take advantage of the critical situation in the Middle East for selfish political ends. That hope had been dashed, said Mr. Loutfi, and he added:

"Furthermore, it is no less strange to find that the French and British Governments are trying of their own accord, unilaterally, to settle a question which has already been brought before the Security Council. That, to our way of thinking, is an entirely unjustifiable infringement of the United Nations Charter. Force may not be used except in accordance with the principles and provisions of the Charter.
The United Kingdom and France have twice made use of the veto to avoid being bound by the decisions of the Council, which might be an inconvenience to them in the aggressive designs they have clearly adopted since Israel launched its armed attack against Egypt."

WAR ON WAR

He said subsequently:

"If France and the United Kingdom go through with the ultimatum they have presented to Egypt, their action will have unforeseeable consequences for which France and the United Kingdom will have to bear the responsibility. In our view, it would be a death-wound to our cherished Organization."

The Soviet representative also touched on the problem of the Security Council's competence. "This ultimatum," he said, "is nothing but a threat of armed intervention by United Kingdom and French forces in the Suez Canal area. It cannot be overlooked that this declaration was made at a moment when it was already known that the Security Council was about to discuss the question of Israel's aggression in Egypt. Accordingly, it was made with the purpose of anticipating Security Council action by means of unilateral action on the part of the Governments of the United Kingdom and France." He then elaborated further:

"It is quite plain that under the United Nations Charter, which was subscribed to by the United Kingdom and France, the Security Council bears the responsibility for the maintenance of peace and security. As we know, the Council has authorized neither the United Kingdom nor France to take any sort of unilateral action, let alone military action, circumventing the United Nations. We are thus confronted with a clear attempt to by-pass the Security Council and to take advantage of the situation created by Israel's aggression in Egypt in order to seize the Suez Canal by armed force."

Mr. Sobolev then said that "it is obvious that this action by the United Kingdom and France is completely incompatible with the United Nations Charter, that it is designed to undermine the authority of the United Nations and, in particular, the Security Council, and that it endangers the maintenance of international peace and security."

The British representative built his defense on the weakness of the Security Council. "Nearly ten years of experience," he said, "have taught the lesson that decisions of this Council, weighty as they are, in regard to Israel and its Arab neighbours are slow to take effect."

Sir Pierson felt that this lesson and the need of action "at once" were sufficient reasons for his and the French Government's steps "of what is certainly a very drastic kind." It was, he said, "preventive action, not just selfishly in our own vital interests, but in the interests of all those who use and are dependent on the Canal and are interested in the maintenance of order in the Middle East." He was very bitter with regard to the attitude of the Soviet Union which "has sought consistently in the last few months to add to the difficulties and dangers of this situation, poses as the protector of the rights of the States in the area and the spokesman of peace." Sir Pierson then added that "but for the unhelpful attitude of the Soviet Union when we were lately discussing the Suez Canal question in this Council, the whole situation in the Middle East would undoubtedly have been far different, and we would probably never have been faced by the grave situation which has arisen."

The French representative simply ignored the competence of the Security Council in restoring the peace. In a very brief statement he dealt with the situation and told the Council that "the French Government considers that the measures it has decided upon, in conjunction with the United Kingdom Government, are such as to avert the danger of hostilities and put an end to the fighting." Consequently, "in these circumstances," said Mr. Louis de Guiringaud, "it would serve no purpose to enter upon a discussion at present of the letter submitted by the representative of Egypt."

The representative of Yugoslavia, Joza Brilej, then suggested "to the members of the Council that they might find time to consider the possibility of calling an emergency session of the General Assembly under the terms of General Assembly resolution 377(V) entitled 'Uniting for Peace.'"

It was not, as he subsequently explained, a formal proposal. It was "just put forward for the consideration of the members of the Council."

* * *

When the Security Council was convened again the next day, October 31, 1956, Mr. Brilej's suggestion had obviously progressed considerably.

The meeting began with a statement by Dag Hammarskjold:

> "I wish to make the following declaration: The principles of the Charter are, by far, greater than the Organization in which they are embodied, and the aims which they are to safeguard are holier than the policies of any single nation or people. As a servant of the Organization, the Secretary-General has the duty to maintain his usefulness by avoiding public stands on conflicts between Member nations unless and until such an action might help to resolve the conflict. However, the discretion and impartiality thus imposed on the Secretary-General by the character of his immediate task may not degenerate into a policy of expediency. He must also be a servant of the principles of the Charter, and its aims must ultimately determine what for him is right and wrong. For that he must stand. A Secretary-General cannot serve on any other assumption than that—within the necessary limits of

THE WAR IN THE MIDDLE EAST 1956

human frailty and honest differences of opinion—all Member nations honour their pledge to observe all Articles of the Charter. He should also be able to assume that those organs which are charged with the task of upholding the Charter will be in a position to fulfill their task."

The Secretary-General obviously felt that war in the Middle East might bring him and the United Nations as a whole in conflict with some members of the Organization. The second great crisis, after Korea, put to a test the usefulness of the United Nations machinery for peace. Inaction in the Middle East was much worse than in Korea because in this new situation not even the first step could be taken. The Security Council was simply by-passed. The assumption "that those organs which are charged with the task of upholding the Charter will be in a position to fulfill their task" already appeared illusory at this moment. There was no way for the Security Council to reach a decision.

Each member of the Security Council expressed, first of all, his confidence in, and high regard for, the Secretary-General. From the very first day, his role became almost tragic. He had "to avoid public stands", be impartial, could not degenerate into expediency, and simultaneously act as the guardian of the pledge of all the nations "to observe all Articles of the Charter"—a herculean task going beyond the possibilities of any individual at a time when the organs of the United Nations were simply paralyzed.

Arkady Sobolev, the Soviet Ambassador, immediately made use of the Franco-British move to show that the two permanent members of the Security Council did not "honour their pledge to observe all articles of the Charter." He said:

WAR ON WAR

"The action of the United Kingdom and France, who have unleashed aggression against Egypt, represents a gross violation of the obligations they have assumed under the United Nations Charter. The Charter requires Members of the United Nations to refrain in their international relations from the threat or use of force. France and the United Kingdom, in their action against Egypt, have not only threatened to use force, but are now bombing Egyptian settlements from the air and are disembarking their armed forces in the territory of Egypt, a Member of the United Nations; that is to say, they are using force in violation of the United Nations Charter. The responsibility of the Governments of the United Kingdom and France for creating an extremely dangerous situation is further increased by the fact that they did not permit the Security Council to perform its duties for the maintenance of international peace laid down in the Charter."

The Soviet representative stressed in his statement time and again that the United Kingdom and France "by-passed the Security Council and violated the standards of international law and the principles of the United Nations." Never before did the Soviet Union have such a strong legal position. However, the Soviet Ambassador did not know what should be done. He mentioned that the Soviet delegation "considers it essential for the Security Council to censure the aggressive action of the United Kingdom and France." This would, of course, not be enough. He subsequently said that the Security Council should "invite" the Governments of the United Kingdom and France to withdraw their armed forces immediately from Egyptian territory. For this purpose, the Soviet delegation would be prepared to submit a draft resolution, "if necessary." Obviously, he knew full well that the two permanent

THE WAR IN THE MIDDLE EAST 1956

members of the Security Council were prepared to vote against such censure and "invitation"; the draft resolution would therefore not have any chance of being accepted. In any event, he said:

> "The Security Council, which bears the primary responsibility for the maintenance of international peace and security, cannot fail to meet its direct and immediate obligations. The peoples of the whole world are awaiting the Security Council's decision."

The Security Council, however, failed to meet its obligation. Sir Pierson Dixon of the United Kingdom and Mr. Louis de Guiringaud of France made it very clear in their remarks that their governments did not intend to yield. They spoke about the very serious situation in the Middle East, about the considerable misunderstanding of their policies, and about the "little practical effect" of the Security Council's decisions "in this area of the globe." Consequently, the two governments had had to take "swift, effective and decisive action." No resolution of censure or "invitation to withdraw" was offered by any member of the Council.

What was offered, was the following draft resolution by Yugoslavia:

> "*The Security Council,*
> *Considering* that a grave situation has been created by action undertaken against Egypt,
> *Taking into account* that the lack of unanimity of its permanent members at the 749th and 750th meetings of the Security Council has prevented it from exercising its primary responsibility for the maintenance of international peace and security,

WAR ON WAR

> *Decides* to call an emergency special session of the General Assembly, as provided in General Assembly resolution 377A (V) of 3 November 1950, in order to make appropriate recommendations."

A tragi-comic situation developed. The matter now under discussion in the Security Council was not, formally, the United States letter of October 29, 1956, but the Egyptian letter of the following day. The vote of the Council (with the veto of France and the United Kingdom) referred to the agenda item "Letter dated 29 October 1956 from the representative of the United States of America" *etc.;* this item was disposed of by the defeat of the American draft resolution. The Security Council subsequently discussed the next item on the agenda; namely "Letter dated 30 October 1956 from the representative of Egypt" *etc*. To this agenda item no resolution was offered. The British and French delegates therefore felt that the main prerequisite for a call for an emergency session of the General Assembly—namely, a lack of unanimity among the permanent members of the Security Council—did not exist.

Sir Pierson Dixon moved to rule the Yugoslavian draft resolution out of order:

> "I submit that the procedure proposed is quite out of order and not in accordance with the clear terms of the 'Uniting for Peace' resolution itself. I shall explain why.
>
> It is quite clear that the 'Uniting for Peace' resolution may be invoked only when certain conditions are fulfilled. The relevant passage of the resolution provides for the calling of an emergency special session of the General Assembly:
>
> '. . . if the Security Council, because of lack of unanimity of the permanent members, fails to exercise its primary responsibility for the maintenance of international peace and

THE WAR IN THE MIDDLE EAST 1956

security in any case where there appears to be a threat to the peace, breach of the peace, or act of aggression . . .'

Thus, a pre-condition of invoking the procedure is that a lack of unanimity of the permanent members of the Security Council should have prevented the Council from taking a decision.

This clearly presupposes that a draft resolution on the substance of the item before the Council has been submitted, circulated and voted upon, and until that has been done, it cannot be determined that the Security Council has failed to take a decision owing to the lack of unanimity of the permanent members. But no such text has been circulated or voted upon on the item now before the Council, namely, the letter dated 30 October from the representative of Egypt."

A legal discussion ensued in order to clarify this matter. In the subsequent vote on the British motion to rule the Yugoslav draft resolution out of order, Australia and Belgium joined the United Kingdom and France, China abstained, and six members (Cuba, Iran, Peru, USSR, United States and Yugoslavia) voted against the United Kingdom motion. The motion was therefore rejected.

The Yugoslav draft resolution was then adopted by seven votes to two. Australia and Belgium abstained, and China voted with the other six members who had voted against the British motion previously.

The very same day telegrams went to all members of the United Nations, calling them to attend the first special emergency session of the General Assembly convened for November 1, 1956, at 5 p.m.

* * *

When the General Assembly met, the first thing done, after the chair had been taken by Mr. Rudecindo Ortega of

Chile was to observe one minute of silence dedicated to prayer or meditation.

Mr. de Guiringaud of France immediately took up the legal point involved in the fact that there was "no manifestation of the lack of unanimity of the permanent members" of the Security Council. The Council could, therefore, not legally bring the Egyptian complaint before the Assembly. He fully reserved his position on the legality of convening the emergency special session of the General Assembly and on all the resolutions which it might subsequently adopt.

In order to avoid further legal disputes, the item proposed for the agenda of the special emergency session was called: "Question considered by the Security Council at its 749th and 750th meetings, held on 30 October 1956."

Sir Pierson Dixon joined his French colleague and repeated his contention made a day before in the Security Council that the convening of the special emergency session of the General Assembly was out of order. "Her Majesty's Government in the United Kingdom," he said, "has nevertheless decided to attend this session." After elaborating on the gravity of the situation in the Middle East, he turned to the history of the problem in the Security Council:

> "Then let us look for a moment at the history of this question in the Security Council. As those representatives who have served in recent years on the Council will know, the Security Council has devoted a very great part of its activities to a continuous effort to uphold the armistice regime and to support the United Nations Chief of Staff. It is my impression—and I should be interested to hear whether my present and past colleagues in the Council disagree with me on this—that the attitude of all the parties has been getting more

THE WAR IN THE MIDDLE EAST 1956

and more refractory, and less and less inclined to take serious account of the Council's views in so far as these seem to them inconvenient.

In these circumstances, how could we have confidence, much as we should have liked to, in view of the past disregard shown by all parties for the United Nations wishes and injunctions and, indeed, disregard for their treaty obligations to one another, that any fresh injunctions by the Security Council would be effective to deal in time—and time was of the essence—with a situation which was getting so clearly out of control?

With regret, I say that the Security Council, in our opinion, could have provided no effective remedy in time."

Sir Pierson continued to attack the Security Council and mentioned that the situation in the Middle East was "not dissimilar to that which obtained at the time of the North Korean invasion." He alluded to the United States action by saying that "on that occasion the Member of the United Nations which had forces on hand and was in a position to intervene at once courageously did so. By a happy chance—and I mean the absence of the Soviet representative from the Security Council on that occasion—the Council was able to endorse the United States action." He then added:

> "The same fortunate chance was not ours. I cannot, however, believe that the United States would not, in any case, have acted, and rightly so, in the circumstances."

The British representative concluded his lengthy statement by stating that if the General Assembly would "merely call upon all parties to cease hostilities and withdraw"—it would mean "the continuation of the chaos in the Middle East."

However, this was precisely what the General Assembly did the next day when it accepted a draft resolution proposed by the American Secretary of State, John Foster Dulles. In this resolution, the General Assembly urged "as a matter of priority that all parties now involved in hostilities in the area agree to an immediate cease-fire and, as part thereof, halt the movement of military forces and arms into the area." It further urged "the parties to the armistice agreements promptly to withdraw all forces behind the armistice lines, to desist from raids across the armistice lines into neighboring territory, and to observe scrupulously the provisions of the armistice agreements."

The General Assembly also suggested "that, upon the cease-fire being effective, steps be taken to reopen the Suez Canal and restore secure freedom of navigation."

Two days later, on November 4, 1956, the General Assembly requested the Secretary-General "to submit to it within forty-eight hours a plan for setting up, with the consent of the nations concerned, of an emergency international United Nations Force to secure and supervise the cessation of hostilities in accordance with all the terms of the aforementioned resolution."

The Secretary-General submitted his first report almost immediately and, on November 5, 1956, the General Assembly established (by Resolution 1000) a United Nations Command for an emergency international force to secure and supervise the cessation of hostilities in accordance with all the terms of the resolution of November 2, 1956.

On November 5, 1956, fighting ceased. On November 6, the Secretary-General submitted his second and final report on

THE WAR IN THE MIDDLE EAST 1956

the plan for an emergency international United Nations Force (Document A/3289). Paragraph 12 of this report gave a clear definition of the functions of the Force:

> "The functions of the United Nations Force would be, when a cease-fire is being established, to enter Egyptian territory with the consent of the Egyptian Government, in order to help maintain quiet during and after the withdrawal of non-Egyptian troops, and to secure compliance with the other terms established in the resolution of 2 November 1956."

On November 7, the General Assembly (in Resolution 1001) approved the guiding principles for the organization and functioning of UNEF (United Nations Emergency Force) as expounded in the Secretary-General's report and particularly concurred with the definition of the functions of UNEF as stated in Paragraph 12 of the report.

The basis for the presence and functioning of UNEF in Egypt was set in an *aide-mémoire* appended to the report of the Secretary-General (Document A/3375) which was approved by the General Assembly on November 24, 1956 (Resolution 1121). The *aide-mémoire* stated:

> "The Government of Egypt and the Secretary-General of the United Nations have stated their understanding on the basic points for the presence and functioning of UNEF as follows:
>
> 1. The Government of Egypt declares that, when exercising its sovereign rights on any matter concerning the presence and functioning of UNEF, it will be guided, in good faith, by its acceptance of General Assembly Resolution 1000 (ES-I) of 5 November 1956.
>
> 2. The United Nations takes note of this declaration of the Government of Egypt and declares that the activities of

WAR ON WAR

UNEF will be guided, in good faith, by the task established for the Force in the aforementioned resolutions; in particular, the United Nations, understanding this to correspond to the wishes of the Government of Egypt, reaffirms its willingness to maintain UNEF *until its task is completed.*

3. The Government of Egypt and the Secretary-General of the United Nations declare that it is their intention to proceed forthwith, in the lights of points 1 and 2 above, to explore jointly concrete aspects of the functioning of UNEF, including its stationing and the question of its lines of communication and supply . . ."

According to this *aide-mémoire,* which, by Resolution 1121 of the General Assembly, was made an official decision of the highest body of the U.N., the UNEF had to be maintained "until its task is completed." It was stated that this corresponded to the wishes of the Government of Egypt; consequently, it had the character of an international agreement which could not be unilaterally changed on any account. Any change in the basic points for the presence and functioning of UNEF would obviously require the consent of the Government of Egypt and of the General Assembly of the United Nations.

CHAPTER THREE

THE WAR IN VIETNAM

THE WAR IN Vietnam—undoubtedly the greatest threat to peace during the sixties—has been of little interest to the United Nations. Yet it has caused enormous destruction, and casualties of this war have numbered into the hundreds of thousands.

"The world has been watching the inexorable escalation of the war in Vietnam with increasing anxiety," U Thant, Secretary-General of the United Nations, said in a speech on May 24, 1966. "Little by little, larger forces and more powerful armaments have been introduced, until an anguished and perplexed world has suddenly found that a limited and local conflict is threatening to turn into a major confrontation."*

Between January 1, 1961 and the middle of May, 1969, 35,265 Americans had been killed and 225,710 wounded, making a total of 260,975 American casualties. During the same period the North Vietnamese lost 500,509 men. The number of South Vietnamese causualties was also enormous.

---

* *The New York Times,* May 25, 1966. (From a speech to the Amalgamated Clothing Workers of America at Atlantic City, made public by the Secretary-General's office).

WAR ON WAR

U Thant further said: "In these grave circumstances, it would appear normal to entrust a world organization such as the United Nations with the task of bringing the parties together to negotiate. Unfortunately, the United Nations is not, at present, so constituted that it could play this role... The United Nations cannot act in a conflict which is beyond its scope..."

This admission on the part of the Secretary-General is the most eloquent indictment of the U.N. Charter. How can the United Nations "maintain international peace and security" (Article 1 of the Charter) if the war in Vietnam is "a conflict beyond its scope"? Are the tens of thousands of casualties not sufficient basis for the Security Council "to determine the existence of any threat to the peace" in Vietnam? (Article 39 of the Charter). Does the open and continuous warfare conducted in a vast territory from Saigon to the Chinese border not warrant "a call upon the parties concerned to comply with such provisional measures as it deems necessary or desirable?" (Article 40 of the Charter).

The Security Council was officially advised of the situation and urged to act by one of its permanent members. On January 31, 1966, the representative of the United States of America wrote to the President of the Security Council.

* * *

Letter dated 31 *January* 1966 *from the Permanent Representative of the United States of America addressed to the President of the Security Council.* (S/7105)

"I have the honour to request that an urgent meeting of the Security Council be called promptly to consider the situation in Vietnam.

"As you know, the United States Government has, time

THE WAR IN VIETNAM

and time again, patiently and tirelessly sought a peaceful settlement of this conflict on the basis of unconditional negotiations and the Geneva Accords of 1954. We have done so both inside and outside of the United Nations.

"In President Johnson's letter of 28 July 1965, to the Secretary-General, in my letter of 30 July 1965 to the President of the Security Council, and in my letter of 4 January 1966 to the Secretary-General, we appealed for whatever help in ending the conflict the Security Council and its members or any other organ of the United Nations might be able to give. We have also been in constant touch with the Secretary-General in order to keep him fully informed and to seek his counsel and assistance. A great number of United Nations Members, acting jointly or separately, have with our earnest encouragement sought to find a means of moving the conflict from the battlefield to the conference table.

"As you are also aware, because my Government was advised by many others that a pause in the bombing of North Vietnam might contribute to the acceptance by its Government of our offer of unconditional negotiations, we did suspend bombing on 24 December and continued that suspension for some thirty-seven days. At the same time, President Johnson dispatched several high-ranking representatives to explain to His Holiness The Pope and to the Chiefs of State or Heads of Government of a number of States our most earnest desire to end the conflict peacefully and promptly. Our views were set forth in fourteen points which were communicated to a very large number of Governments and later published and which were summarized in the third paragraph of my letter of 4 January 1966 to the Secretary-General.

"I should like to repeat that summary to you as follows:

WAR ON WAR

'That the United States is prepared for discussions or negotiations without any prior conditions whatsoever or on the basis of the Geneva Accords of 1954 and 1962, that a reciprocal reduction of hostilities could be envisaged and that a cease-fire might be the first order of business in any discussions or negotiations, that the United States remains prepared to withdraw its forces from South Viet-Nam as soon as South Viet-Nam is in a position to determine its own future without external interference, that the United States desires no continuing military presence or bases in Viet-Nam, that the future political structure in South Viet-Nam should be determined by the South Viet-Namese people themselves through democratic processes, and that the question of the reunification of the two Viet-Nams should be decided by the free decision of their two peoples.'

"Subsequently, the President in his State of the Union Address on 12 January once again reiterated the willingness of the United States to consider at a conference or in other negotiations any proposals which might be put forward by others. I am authorized to inform the Council that these United States views were transmitted both directly and indirectly to the Government of North Vietnam and were received by that Government.

"Unhappily, there has been no affirmative response whatsoever from Hanoi to our efforts to bring the conflict to the negotiating table, to which so many Governments lent their sympathy and assistance. Instead, there have been from Hanoi, and of course from Peking as well, merely the familiar charges that our peace offensive, despite the prolonged bombing pause, was merely a 'fraud' and a 'swindle' deserving no serious consideration. The most recent response seemed to be that set forth in President Ho Chi Minh's letter to certain Heads

THE WAR IN VIETNAM

of State which was broadcast from Hanoi on 28 January. In this letter President Ho Chi Minh made quite clear his unwillingness at this time to proceed with unconditional negotiations; on the contrary, he insisted on a number of preconditions which would in effect require the United States to accept Hanoi's solution before negotiations had even begun. This is obviously unacceptable.

"Therefore, Mr. President, my Government has concluded that it should now bring this problem with all its implications for peace formally before the Security Council. We are mindful of the discussions over the past months among the members of the Council as to whether a formal meeting could usefully be held in the context of other efforts then in train. We are also aware that it may not be easy for the Council itself, in view of all the obstacles, to take constructive action on this question. We are firmly convinced, however, that in the light of its obligations under the Charter to maintain international peace and security and the failure so far of all efforts outside the United Nations to restore peace, the Council should address itself urgently and positively to this situation and exert its most vigorous endeavours and its immense prestige to finding a prompt solution to it.

"We hope that the members of the Security Council will agree that our common dedication to peace and our common responsibility for the future of mankind require no less. In this connection, we are mindful of the renewed appeal of His Holiness The Pope only two days ago in which he suggested that 'an arbitration of the United Nations confided to neutral nations might tomorrow—we would like to hope even today—resolve this terrible question.'

"Accept, etc.

(*Signed*) Arthur J. Goldberg

WAR ON WAR

* * *

Speaking at the meeting of the Security Council a day after the dispatch of this letter—on February 1, 1966—the representative of the United States stressed once again that "there is no more urgent task confronting the statesmen of the world and the Security Council as well as the United Nations as a whole, than that of finding first a way to terminate the fighting in Vietnam, and then a settlement which will bring enduring peace to the Vietnamese people."

The ensuing discussion, however, clearly showed that there was considerable opposition to placing the war in Vietnam on the agenda of the Security Council.

The representative of the Union of Soviet Socialist Republics (Mr. Fedorenko) said: "The Soviet delegation deems it essential to state that it objects to the convening of the Security Council for the discussion of the question of Vietnam and declares itself to be against the inclusion of the present item in the agenda of the Security Council." He then went on to say: "The Soviet Union, as is known, supports the just position of the Government of the Democratic Republic of Vietnam that the Vietnamese question should be settled within the framework of the Geneva Accords. It is clear to all that the proposal of the United States of America, regarding the consideration of the question of Vietnam in the Security Council, is not at all aimed towards a genuine settlement of the question of Vietnam, but is only a diversionary tactic undertaken in order to cover—by means of talks regarding a so-called settlement in Vietnam—the measures of the Pentagon to expand its aggressive war."

The representative of France (Mr. Seydoux) said: "My Government does not believe that the United Nations constitutes the proper framework for achieving a peaceful solution

THE WAR IN VIETNAM

of the Vietnam conflict. This position is based upon two essential reasons. On the one hand, the principal parties involved in this conflict, with the exception of one of them, are not represented in our Organization. China is not represented in any authentic way, while the two Vietnams are not Members of the United Nations. Even on the assumption that the Council might agree to request the two Governments to appear before it, the discussions that would ensue here would not take place on a footing of equality between the two parties, which is the very foundation of any healthy and fruitful negotiation. A debate before the Security Council might run the risk of resulting ultimately—as has happened in the past—only in a vain confrontation and in demonstrations of purely formal character. On the other hand—and I might say especially—it might well be disputed that the International Organization is empowered to discuss a question which formerly was settled within the framework of the Geneva Conference, and which remains within the competence thereof . . . The intervention of the United Nations at the present stage, apart from the objections to which I referred a moment ago, would, in our opinion, but add to the existing confusion. In the absence of a real discussion between the parties essentially involved, it could but lead to misunderstanding. These are the reasons for which it will not be possible for my delegation—which is as aware as any other of the dangers to peace—to support the request of which we are seized to inscribe the question of Vietnam on our agenda."

The representative of the United Kingdom supported the United States. "Even having heard," he said, "what the representative of the Soviet Union put to us, I do not believe that any of us will have any doubt that we should proceed to discuss in this Council this most vital and dangerous matter. I do not believe that there is any doubt anywhere about the dangers posed to peace in Asia and beyond by the situation in Vietnam. I do not believe that there is any doubt anywhere about the obligations of this Council under the Charter for the maintenance of international peace and security. I do not believe that there is any doubt that the Security Council should not shirk its duty, however difficult it may be. Consequently my delegation fully supports the United States Government's action in making the approach which it has now made to the Security Council."

Other members of the Security Council, however, expressed doubts. "Without going into a substance of the problem," said Mr. Coulibaly, the representative of the African Republic of Mali, "my delegation believes that so important a question, which has a direct bearing on international peace and security, should be discussed in an atmosphere of serenity and by means of arrangements which would place the parties concerned on an equal footing to express and defend their points of view. But these conditions do not exist in the United Nations or in the Security Council, where only one of the interested parties is represented. At the present stage of the development of the question of Vietnam, the Security Council does not seem to be the most effective and appropriate body in which to discuss the subject . . . Since the parties which are suffering the most cruelly from the Vietnam conflict have made known their opposition to any discussion of the question in the United Nations, I can see no useful purpose in beginning a debate in the Security Council now on that problem . . . My delegation believes that, if they are to be effective, the interventions of the Security Council must be timely and must be carried out in conditions assuring their complete success." He concluded by stating "that the delegation of Mali is opposed to the exam-

THE WAR IN VIETNAM

ination of the question of Vietnam by the Security Council at the present stage in the development of the conflict."

The representative of Nigeria (Chief Adebo) stated that he wished "to make it abundantly clear that we do not at all condemn the United States delegation for bringing this matter to the notice of the Security Council," but that Nigeria would abstain from voting.

The representative of Uganda (Mr. Kironde) said that his delegation "has no intention of siding with one or other of the big Powers." He wondered whether any useful purpose would be served by pushing the issue to the vote and asked the chairman: "Would it not be enough, Mr. President, if you, in your wisdom, were to conclude the debate, summarizing it as best you can, bringing out the points of agreement and of disagreement, and let it go at that?"

The representative of Bulgaria (Mr. Tarabanov) accused the United States of wishing "to utilize the debates in the Security Council as a smoke screen behind which it wants to conceal its crimes; it wishes to show that there was no alternative but to intensify the war of aggression against the people of all Vietnam." He quoted Secretary-General U Thant who said, on January 20, 1966:

> ". . . It is true that the United Nations has a primary responsibility to maintain international peace and security. It was true in 1954 as it is true in 1966. Now look at the situation in 1954. The parties to the conflict decided to resolve their differences in Geneva, outside the framework of the United Nations. Of course, a lot of thought was given to the prospective United Nations involvement even at that time. But the big Powers, plus the parties to the conflict, decided that the discussions should take outside the framework of the United Nations . . .

WAR ON WAR

If it was true that the discussions on the Viet-Nam situation could take place in Geneva in 1954, outside the framework of the United Nations, the same considerations still apply today, because some of the parties primarily involved in the conflict are still not members of the United Nations. This is the gravest impediment to any United Nations involvement in finding a peaceful solution to the Viet-Nam conflict."

Mr. Tarabanov felt that involvement at this time might be a "hasty and untimely intervention on the part of the Security Council." He "resolutely" opposed "the inscription on the agenda of the question proposed by the United States, namely, the question of the situation in Vietnam."

Even those who favored the inscription of the United States proposal on the agenda were skeptical over the role of the Security Council in the settlement of the conflict. Frank H. Corner of New Zealand stated that he did not envisage, "nor do our colleagues, that the Council itself should necessarily be regarded as an appropriate vehicle for negotiation." However, he asked: "Are we going to adopt the attitude that we have nothing to say, or that it is improper, whatever political and well-known difficulties may be in the way, for the Council to discuss the question and to see whether there may be avenues showing promise of assisting in its solution?"

Dr. J.G. de Beus of the Netherlands made an attempt to analyze the objections interposed against debating the Vietnam question in the Security Council. The first objection was that not all the countries involved were members of the United Nations. That, he said, could not be a determining factor against discussion in the Council since, under the Charter, the United Nations was to ensure that the States which were not members of the United Nations should respect the principles

THE WAR IN VIETNAM

of the Charter regarding the maintenance of international peace. The second claim made was that the problem should be solved in the context not of the United Nations, but of the Geneva Conference of 1954. With that point of view he basically agreed, but he felt that "the purpose of the discussion was not to resolve the problem within the context of the United Nations but to arrange a pre-conference looking towards the application of the Geneva Accords of 1954 and 1962." The third argument asserted was that the situation created by the resumption of bombings of North Vietnam was hardly propitious for fruitful debate. This objection was not valid, because, Dr. de Beus said, on the contrary, these developments made it all the more imperative that the subject be discussed. "If events," he said, "are allowed to run their course, a further escalation of the war to ever-bigger proportions seems inevitable."

Arthur J. Goldberg of the United States and Nikolai T. Fedorenko of the Soviet Union then made their final statements. Goldberg paid tribute to the wisdom of the new and old members of the Security Council, "aligned and nonaligned." First he dealt with the argument that the Geneva Conference provided the only proper international body to handle the problem of Vietnam. "The United States," he said, "has no quarrel with this contention... Let the joint chairmen (i.e. the United Kingdom and the Soviet Union) issue the call today, and we will be in Geneva tomorrow at a conference, and then indeed there will be no necessity for the Security Council to deal with this matter." Goldberg pointed out that it was the Soviet Union which had refused "to join in any steps to reconvene the Conference." He made it clear that "under these circumstances, the choice before us members of the Security Council is not whether to deal with this problem in the Council, or to deal with it in Geneva, but whether to deal with it at all. The door to Geneva is, at least for the time being, closed, and the question we have to decide is a plain and simple one: do we wish also to close the door to the United Nations? What will the people of the world say if we do?"

Concerning the second point advanced by the opponents of the inclusion of the Vietnam problem in the agenda of the Security Council—that several of the parties to the conflict were not members of the United Nations—Goldberg quoted Article 32 of the Charter which stated that "any State which is a Member of the United Nations, if it is a party to a dispute under consideration by the Security Council, shall be invited to participate, without vote, in the discussion relating to the dispute." The United Nations had considered in the past, and presumably would do so in the future, matters in which members or non-members had refused to participate.

Goldberg also rejected the suggestion that "the Council should not attempt to deal with the problem unless it is assured that it can do so successfully." He pointed out that "the Council has not been inhibited in the past from dealing with threats to the peace of the world because it could not be assured of doing so successfully." He asked, "Were the Council to refuse even to attempt to carry out the obligations laid upon it by the Charter, what credit and what prestige could it hope to have in the world?"

The U.S. representative said that he completely failed to understand how those States which repeatedly insisted that the Security Council, and the Security Council alone, had the responsibility for the maintenance of international peace and security, could now deny its competence. He then made the following significant statement:

THE WAR IN VIETNAM

"Permit me to say most solemnly to my fellow members of the Council at this critical juncture of its history that what is at stake here is not the United States position; we have brought the matter to the Council. What is at stake here is the matter of how the world will judge the Council if it refuses even to discuss and consider that problem which public opinion almost everywhere considers to be the most serious threat to the peace now confronting mankind. What reliance, what confidence will the peoples of the world henceforth place in the Security Council—in the United Nations itself—if we adjourn without having made an attempt to deal with this matter?"

Nikolai T. Fedorenko, the Soviet representative, reacted by saying that "the representative of the United States did not produce anything new in substance and he was, of course, unsuccessful in making any more attractive the farce that is being played out by the United States at the present time." He accused Goldberg of "a distortion of the actual state of affairs" with regard to the Geneva Conference. When the Geneva Accords were reached in 1954, he said, "there was not a single American soldier in Vietnam." The present situation is quite different: "South Vietnam has been completely taken over by the United States interventionist hordes."

Fedorenko did not discuss the legal arguments made by Goldberg, but quoted in full a message sent by Chairman Podgorny of the Presidium of the USSR to President Ho Chi Minh of North Vietnam. In this message Podgorny said:

"Dear Comrade Ho Chi Minh . . . The Soviet people fully share the wrath of the Vietnamese people with respect to the aggressive actions of the United States of America and resolutely condemn the armed intervention of the United States

WAR ON WAR

against the southern portion of your country and against the sovereign socialist State, the Democratic Republic of Vietnam. The despatch of American troops to South Vietnam, and the use by them of napalm bombs and poisonous substances against the South Vietnamese population, the bombing of the Democratic Republic of Vietnam and the violation of its air space, constitute acts of aggression and the flouting of the standards of international law and the Geneva Accords of 1954...

"The United States of America, while resorting to various political manoeuvres, is unwilling to accept the just demands of the Vietnamese people...

"(The United States) is unwilling to recognize the National Liberation Front as the genuine representative of the population of South Vietnam and is unwilling to conduct negotiations with it. Instead of unconditionally and for all time putting an end to its piratical raids upon the territory of the Democratic Republic of Vietnam, the United States of America has accompanied the temporary cessations of such raids with ultimatums addressed to the Democratic Republic of Vietnam. The resumption by the United States air forces of the barbarous bombings of the Democratic Republic of Vietnam has bared to the eyes of the whole world the falsity of the so-called 'peace offensive' of the United States..."

Fedorenko concluded by stating that he objected to the convening of the Security Council for the purpose of discussing the Vietnam question. "We declare ourselves," he said, "to be against the inclusion of this item in the agenda of the Council."

* * *

The decision on the adoption of the agenda was postponed until the next day.

THE WAR IN VIETNAM

On February 2, 1966, the representatives of the USSR and the United States resumed their debate. Fedorenko said that "the delegation of the Soviet Union deems it necessary once more to affirm most vigorously its objection to the convening of the Security Council for the purpose of discussing the question of Vietnam and declares itself opposed to the inclusion of this question on the agenda of the Council".

He quoted an appeal of President Ho Chi Minh of January 24, 1966:

> "It is crystal clear that the United States is the aggressor who is trampling underfoot the Vietnamese soil. The people of South Vietnam are the victims of aggression and are fighting in self-defence. If the United States really wants peace it must recognize the National Front for the Liberation of South Vietnam as the sole genuine representative of the people of South Vietnam, and engage in direct negotiations with it."

The USSR representative advised the Security Council that the National Liberation Front of South Vietnam had that very day published a statement "in reply to the decision of the United States of America to bring the problem of Vietnam to the Security Council"

> "In that statement it is pointed out that the Security Council has no right to take any decisions on questions involving South Vietnam and that all resolutions of the Security Council on the question of Vietnam will be null and void as far as the National Liberation Front is concerned."

Fedorenko expressed "astonishment at the hypocritical behaviour of the United States" and said further:

> "The plan for torpedoing the basis of the Geneva Agree-

ments is being represented as peaceful action on the part of the United States through its initiative in convening the Security Council . . . In the present situation we deem it essential to express the hope that members of the Council will not follow in the wake of those who, speculating upon the striving of peoples towards peace, are in fact trying to achieve a sort of indulgence in advance for continuing the escalation of their aggressive war in Viet-Nam . . ."

Ambassador Goldberg stated that he would reply in detail on a later occasion. He rejected Fedorenko's accusation that the United States had violated the Geneva Accords. He quoted a statement made by the United States at the time of the adoption of the Geneva Accords to the effect that "the United States would view any renewal of the aggression in violation of the aforesaid agreements with grave concern and as seriously threatening international peace and security." Subsequently, the International Commission for Supervision and Control in Vietnam, in its Special Report dated June 2, 1962, confirmed "that in specific instances there is evidence to show that armed and unarmed personnel, arms, munitions and other supplies have been sent from the Zone in the North to the Zone in the South with the object of supporting, organizing and carrying out hostile activities, including armed attacks, directed against the Armed Forces and Administration of the Zone in the South." The same report confirmed that the regular forces of North Vietnam had "allowed the Zone in the North to be used for inciting, encouraging and supporting hostile activities in the Zone in the South, aimed at the overthrow of the Administration in the South." All these activities were in violation of the Agreement on the cessation of hostilities in Vietnam.

Goldberg concluded his statement by saying that "one of

THE WAR IN VIETNAM

the purposes of the United States in coming to the Council is not to conceal facts but to expose to the sunlight of this Council's proceedings what the real facts are."

Fedorenko took the floor again in order "once again to confirm the position stated by us a moment ago, and once again to indicate that it is precisely the United States of America that bears the full weight of responsibility for the violation of the Geneva Accords."

The vote was finally taken. Nine members of the Security Council (Argentina, China, Japan, Jordan, Netherlands, New Zealand, United Kingdom, United States, Uruguay) voted for the adoption of the agenda. Two (Bulgaria and USSR) voted against. Four (France, Mali, Nigeria, Uganda) abstained. The agenda was adopted as suggested by the United States.

* * *

After this long struggle, no meeting of the Security Council was called to discuss the Vietnam problem. At the end of the meeting of February 2, 1966, the President suggested and the Council agreed to hold "informal and private consultations in order to decide on the most effective and appropriate way of continuing the debate in the future." These consultations produced no results. Accordingly, Akira Matsui, the President of the Security Council for the month of February, sent a letter to the members of the Council, in which he reported that "serious differences remained unsolved, especially as to whether consideration of the problem of Vietnam in the forum of the Council would be useful under the circumstances." He also reported that some members, in conformity with the position they had taken during the debate, had not participated in the consultations. Mr. Matsui felt that it would be inopportune for the Council to hold a further debate at the time.

Matsui made some comments on the essence of the problem which had serious repercussions. He wrote that he could detect a certain degree of common feeling among many members of the Council. "There was general grave concern and growing anxiety over the continuation of hostilities in Vietnam and a strong desire for the early cessation of hostilities and a peaceful solution of the Vietnam problem. There appeared also to be a feeling that the termination of the conflict in Vietnam should be sought through negotiations in an appropriate forum in order to work out the implementation of the Geneva Accords."

The letter of the President of the Security Council was circulated as a Security Council document (S/7168) under date of February 26, 1966. It immediately stirred up a hornet's nest. On February 28, 1966, M. Roger Seydoux, the representative of France, submitted a letter (S/7173) stating that there had been no substantive discussion in the Council and that informal and private consultations could not take the place of such discussions. Therefore, he said, it was inappropriate to put forward any conclusion regarding the feeling of the Security Council or of any of its members.

A day later, on March 1, 1966, Nikolai T. Fedorenko, the Soviet representative, addressed a letter to the President of the Security Council (S/7175), in which he stated that the action taken by Mr. Matsui had produced strong objections since the Council had not instructed the President to make any statements and the latter could not, therefore, send such a letter in his capacity as President of the Security Council. Fedorenko claimed that this action went beyond the limits of the President's jurisdiction, violated the Security Council's

THE WAR IN VIETNAM

rules of procedure and could only be regarded as a blatant attempt to support the maneuver of the United States. The USSR therefore considered that the President's statement was illegal and had no legal force whatsoever.

Mr. Tarabanov of Bulgaria went a step further. On March 3 he sent a letter to the President of the Security Council (S/7174), in which he noted that since no substantive debate had taken place in the Council and since the problem could not be solved within the United Nations, the Council had not authorized its President to draw conclusions or to sum up the feeling of its members in an official document. The Bulgarian delegation therefore considered it necessary to return the letter addressed to it by the President on February 26, 1966.

The representative of Mali, Sori Coulibaly, sent a letter to the President of the Council, dated March 2, in which he declared that he wished to enter the most express reservations regarding both the principle and the motives of the letter of the President of February 26, especially in view of the fact that the meetings held on February 1 and 2 had been devoted to procedural discussions relating solely to the adoption of the agenda. As no discussion had been held on the question, there could be no grounds for discussing any conclusions. The communication dated February 26, 1966 could not constitute a valid precedent in the practice of the Security Council. (S/7176).

* * *

The next document in the files of the Security Council relating to Vietnam is a letter of June 30, 1966 from Ambassador Goldberg to the President of the Security Council. (S/7391).

WAR ON WAR

In this letter, which was circulated as a Security Council document, Goldberg informed the President of the Council that his Government had been required to take further steps to counter and limit the increased intensity of North Vietnam's aggression against the Republic of Vietnam. In view of a substantial increase in the level of infiltration of armed men and war supplies from North Vietnam into South Vietnam, and the importance of petroleum products to the infiltrators, the United States had felt compelled to send its aircraft to attack the largest petroleum facilities in North Vietnam; *i.e.*, those located near Hanoi and Haiphong. Further evidence of this conduct could be found in the construction by North Vietnam, often outside its own borders, of new routes and the improvement of existing ones, all designed to facilitate infiltration by truck into South Vietnam in all types of weather. Goldberg said that every effort had been made to prevent harm to civilians and to avoid destruction of non-military facilities. It was a tragedy that repeated efforts to open negotiations had been answered from North Vietnam by an increase in the tempo of its military build-up and operations. The United States objectives in Vietnam were limited: it did not seek to change or destroy the Government of North Vietnam or its people. It did not wish to turn South Vietnam into a permanent ally of the West, nor did it seek to establish permanent military bases there. It sought only to afford the people of South Vietnam the opportunity to shape their own destiny free of coercion. The United States had learned from two aerial bombing pauses that it was not enough to stop the bombing over North Vietnam while other military operations continued. It was the war, not just the bombing, that should come to an end.

When this letter reached the members of the United Nations, the reaction that followed was similar to the frustrat-

THE WAR IN VIETNAM

ing discussion in the Security Council in the beginning of February.

Three identical letters, dated July 11, were addressed to the President of the Security Council by the representatives of the USSR, the Byelorussian SSR and the Ukrainian SSR. (S/7401, S/7402 and S/7403). In these letters it was alleged that the Government of the United States had embarked on a course of expanding the shameful war against the Democratic Republic of Vietnam and the Vietnamese people as a whole. The letter stated that the United States was intensifying the publicity campaign about its desire for a "peaceful settlement" at the very moment when, by carrying out barbaric bombing attacks on the Hanoi and Haiphong areas, it had expanded its aggression in Vietnam and utterly exposed its real objectives. The representatives of the USSR, the Byelorussian SSR and the Ukrainian SSR resolutely condemned the "aggressive" actions of the United States in Vietnam and stressed that the way to peace in that country lay through the cessation of United States "aggression" and intervention in the internal affairs of the Vietnamese people.

A day later, July 12, 1966, the representative of Bulgaria addressed a letter to the President of the Security Council (S/7407), referring also to the June 30 communication of the United States representative and asserting that the letter was merely a new maneuver relying upon hypocritical declarations in favor of peace to cover and justify the expansion of the war in Vietnam. The recent air raids on Hanoi and Haiphong proved once more, the Bulgarian letter said, the flagrant violation of the 1954 Geneva Agreements by the United States. The only way for the United States to prevent a major disaster was not to send such "explanatory" letters but, *inter alia*, to

WAR ON WAR

put an end to its aggressive war, stop the air raids in the North, and withdraw its forces from the South.

All four representatives returned the letter of the United States representative of June 30, which had been circulated as a Security Council document.

Meanwhile, the greedy vampire of war continued to devour countless victims.

CHAPTER FOUR

WAR IN THE MIDDLE EAST 1967

ON MAY 18, 1967, at 12 noon, the Secretary-General of the United Nations received the following message from the Minister for Foreign Affairs of the United Arab Republic (the formal designation of Egypt since February 1, 1958):

> "The Government of the United Arab Republic has the honour to inform Your Excellency that it has decided to terminate the presence of the United Nations Emergency Force from the territory of the United Arab Republic and Gaza strip.
> Therefore, I request that the necessary steps be taken for the withdrawal of the Force as soon as possible.
> I avail myself of this opportunity to express to Your Excellency my gratitude and warm regards."

U Thant answered the same day, in the early evening of May 18, that the U.A.R. request would be complied with and that he was proceeding with the issuance of instructions for the necessary arrangements to be put in train without delay for the orderly withdrawal of the Force. The Secretary-General immediately reported this development in Document A/6669. In the course of his discussion, U Thant mentioned that he had drawn the attention of the U.A.R. to the *aide-mémoire* of 1956 concerning the activities of UNEF; he did, however, not advert to whether the *aide-mémoire* (discussed at the conclusion of Chapter Two) could lawfully have been revoked unilaterally by the U.A.R. before the task of UNEF had been "completed," although that was the time limit imposed by the United Nations on the maintenance of UNEF, with the clear consent of the Government of Egypt.

On May 19, the Secretary-General sent an alarming report to the Security Council (S/7896) "in order to convey to the members of the Council his deep anxiety about recent developments in the Near East." He concluded this report with the warning that, in his opinion, the current situation in the Near East had become more disturbing, indeed more menacing, than at any time since the fall of 1956. He then left for Cairo to discuss the situation with the Government of the U.A.R.

On May 23, 1967, George Ignatieff, Representative of Canada, and Hans Tabor, Representative of Denmark, addressed the following letter to the President of the Security Council:

> "We have the honour to request an urgent meeting of the Security Council to consider the extremely grave situation in the Middle East which is threatening international peace and security.
>
> In his report to the Security Council of 19 May 1967, the Secretary-General has conveyed his 'deep anxiety about recent developments in the Near East' and what he considers to be 'an increasingly dangerous deterioration along the borders there.' He also warned the Council that the current situation in the Near East 'is more disturbing, indeed, I may

say more menacing, than at any time since the fall of 1956.'

Since the Secretary-General's report was issued, developments have taken place which have caused the situation to deteriorate further.

We have concluded, therefore, that the time has come for the Security Council, which has a primary responsibility for the maintenance of international peace and security, to discharge its responsibilities. We believe that action by the Security Council would reinforce the current efforts being made by the Secretary-General to preserve peace in the area. It is of course also of the utmost importance that no Member State of the United Nations take any action which would worsen the situation."

Upon receipt of this letter, the President of the Security Council, (during the month of May 1967 this was the representative of China), called a meeting for May 24.

At the opening of the session, the representative of the Soviet Union stated that "the Soviet delegation deems it necessary to stress that it does not see sufficient grounds for such a hasty convening of the Security Council and the artificially dramatic climate fostered by the representatives of some Western Powers, which are probably counting on an exaggerated effort in the staging of this meeting."

The representative of Canada, in his reply, again quoted the alarming report of the Secretary-General, who just had left for the Middle East in order to preserve peace in the area. "In the face of the grave facts," he asked, "in the face of the mounting threats and the *faits accomplis*, how can the international community discharge its collective duty unless the full influence of the Security Council, which is charged under Article 24 of the Charter with primary responsibility for the maintenance of international peace and security precisely 'to ensure prompt and effective action'—I underline those words—is brought to bear upon the seriously deteriorating situation in the Middle East?"

The representative of the Soviet Union, however, felt that the representative of Canada "instead of speaking to the substance of our remarks, engaged in disquisitions on the substance of the problem, all of which is contrary to the procedure customarily followed in the Security Council." In his opinion, "information must necessarily first be received regarding the mission undertaken by the Secretary-General." He concluded by saying that "all this sounds rather ironical and reminds us of an Oriental proverb: You show him the moon but all he looks at is your finger."

The representatives of Mali, Bulgaria, India, France, Ethiopia, and Nigeria also felt that it might have been better to delay the meeting until after a report was received from the Secretary-General on his visit to the United Arab Republic. The representative of the United States, on the other hand, said that "this Council would be burying its head in the sand if it refused to recognize the threat to peace implicit in the developments which have occurred since the Secretary-General left New York two days ago." He felt that "this Council meeting cannot dramatize a situation which at this moment is at the centre of the stage of world concern. It can, however, play a role in drawing the curtain on a tragedy which potentially threatens the peace and well-being of all the people in the area and, indeed, of all mankind."

No vote was taken by the Security Council but the agenda—the subject of the letter by the representatives of Canada and Denmark—was adopted without formal protest. The representatives of Israel and the United Arab Republic were

THE WAR IN THE MIDDLE EAST 1967

invited to take seats at the Council table, and the Security Council began to discuss the situation in the Middle East.

The representative of Denmark referred to the sudden withdrawal of the United Nations Emergency Force from the territory of the United Arab Republic. This development, which had taken place on May 18, had, in the words of the Secretary-General in his report to the General Assembly, restored "the armed confrontation of the United Arab Republic and Israel" and had removed "the stabilizing influence of an international force operating along the boundaries between the two nations." He went on to say:

> "We do not wish to dramatize the situation, but I dare say that this is not necessary because, since the beginning of the withdrawal of the UNEF, the situation along the borders between Israel and the United Arab Republic has been constantly deteriorating, and at an alarming speed. There has been a military build-up along the borders of Israel and the United Arab Republic, and there is no way of denying that the stage is set for a major military clash. The development has now reached a point where it seems as if the slightest miscalculation, the slightest misunderstanding of one or the other side of the opponent's intentions, could lead to large-scale hostilities.
>
> "It was our hope that U Thant's decision to go to the area would in itself have had a pacifying effect. However, we have to admit that the urgency and the danger of the situation have become even more obvious since then. Only two days ago the President of the United Arab Republic declared that Israel ships and other ships carrying certain cargoes to Israel would be prevented from passing through the Strait of Tiran, and the Israel Government on its side has stressed that it would consider such a move as an attack.
>
> "Now what should be our attitude in the face of this grave

danger? Should the Council just stand by, see what happens and hope for the best? That is hardly, I believe, what world public opinion would expect of us . . . It is fortunate, indeed, that the confrontation between the parties has so far not gone beyond the level of mutually hostile declarations, but let us not forget that the most important task of this Council is the preservation, not the restoration, of international peace and security."

In the discussion that followed, various representatives expressed their concern about the highly explosive situation in the Middle East. The representative of the United States quoted President Johnson's statement of May 23, 1967, to the effect that "the United States is firmly committed to the support of the political independence and territorial integrity of all the nations in the area. The United States strongly opposes aggression by anyone in the area, in any form, overt or clandestine." The representative of the United States interrupted the quotation after the word "all" to say: "and I emphasize 'all'." He mentioned that "in the Suez crisis we stood against old allies" and stressed again "the vital interest which all the Powers, great and small alike, share in maintaining an impartial international instrument of stability—an instrument which, when danger and discord arise, can transcend narrow self-interest and put power at the service of peace; that instrument is the United Nations, and above all it is this Security Council, with its primary Charter responsibility for the maintenance of international peace and security."

Other speakers, representing Japan, Canada, France, United Kingdom, advised caution and moderation. The representative of the United Kingdom said "a very friendly word to the representative of the Soviet Union." He said that the Soviet representative's "motives are always crystal clear; indeed, his motives are as transparent as his proverbs are obscure." The Soviet representative replied that "despite the British sense of humour, our British colleague did not show any smile on his face. He probably remembered a recent statement made in the General Assembly by one of our friends, who said that when the lion bares his fangs, it is unreasonable to suppose that he is smiling. It may be, of course, that this is due to a lack in education or in upbringing, but all of us have our defects and our shortcomings. It happens that even monkeys fall from trees."

After this recourse to Oriental wisdom, the USSR representative quoted a statement by his government, dated May 23, 1967, in which Israel was warned that it "will bear the responsibility for the consequences of its aggressive policy." The representatives of the United Arab Republic and of Israel exchanged accusations. The representative of the United States then made a brief statement:

> "Ambassador Fedorenko made some remarks describing the alleged role of the United States in the present Middle Eastern crisis. In reply to this, I would only remind him of the famous story of 'Alice in Wonderland.' I am sure you will remember what Alice told the White Queen in 'Through the Looking Glass': that one cannot believe impossible things. To that the White Queen replied: 'I dare say you have not had much practice. When I was your age, I always did it for half an hour a day. Why, sometimes I believed as many as six impossible things before breakfast.' "

The representative of the Soviet Union answered immediately:

> "We had no desire to continue these polemics, but when somebody speaks about us, we always consider it impolite not to answer. And since my colleague, Mr. Goldberg, related to

the Council a very old tale concerning Wonderland and its naive protagonists, we would like to say that, of course, those who attended primary school know that story. This is indeed a very old-fashioned way to look at a mirror . . . One does not quite understand the conclusion of the representative of the United States. His statement was somewhat nebulous. However, any fable has a moral, and those who continued their studies at a higher level after primary school have probably also studied history. Many people may recall the story of the student who asked his teacher, an ancient sage: 'What must we do, how are we to behave, when we commit a given act?' That wise old man—he was also from the Orient—answered: 'Do not forget to look back in order to understand your actions better.' "

This exchange of fables and parables resulted in no decision whatever. The President of the Council suggested adjournment in order to facilitate informal consultation among the members. Some representatives felt, however, that such consultations were undesirable. One representative called the whole debate an "exercise in futility" which "has contributed nothing to clarifying the question of the Middle East." Finally, the meeting adjourned without any decision having been taken.

U Thant returned from his visit to Cairo and on May 26, submitted to the Security Council a report on his trip. He reiterated the assessment he had made in his previous report on May 19. The Secretary-General objected to the allegation that the withdrawal of the UNEF was the primary cause of the crisis in the Middle East. In his opinion, the decision of the United Arab Republic to restrict shipping in the Strait of Tiran had created a new situation. "Free passage through the Strait was one of the questions which Israel considered most

THE WAR IN THE MIDDLE EAST 1967

vital to its interests. The position of the U.A.R. was that the Strait was territorial waters in which it had a right to control shipping; Israel contested that position and asserted the right of innocent passage through the Strait. Furthermore, Israel had declared that it would regard the closing of the Strait of Tiran to Israel flagships and any restrictions on cargoes of ships of other flags proceeding to Israel as a *casus belli*." U Thant further stated that, while in Cairo, he had called to the attention of the Government of the U.A.R. the dangerous consequences which could ensue from restricting the innocent passage of ships in the Strait of Tiran. He had received assurances that the U.A.R. would not initiate offensive action against Israel. U Thant pointed out that a legal controversy had existed prior to 1956 as to the extent of the right of innocent passage by commercial vessels through the Strait of Tiran and the Gulf of Aqaba. As long as UNEF forces were stationed at Sharm El Sheikh and Ras Nasrani, at the entrance of the Gulf of Aqaba, there had been no interference with shipping in the Strait of Tiran. In view, however, of the conflicting stands taken by the U.A.R. and Israel, the situation in the Strait of Tiran represented a serious potential threat to peace. In addition, other problems, "such as sabotage and terrorist activities and rights of cultivation in disputed areas in the demilitarized zone between Israel and Syria" could cause a clash between Israel and her neighbors and this "would inevitably set off a general conflict in the Middle East." The Secretary-General therefore suggested a "breathing spell" which would allow tension to subside from its explosive level."

The Security Council met on May 27, 1967 and discussed the Secretary General's report. All speakers endorsed his appeal for a breathing spell. Ambassador Goldberg of the United States was rather optimistic with regard to the role of the United Nations in the crisis. "In dealing with this problem," he said, "we should at all costs avoid wasteful recriminations over the response of the United Nations to recent events. The Organization has played a crucial role for many years in maintaining peace, however fragile, in the Near East. The General Armistice Agreements, the Truce Supervision Organization, the admirable ten-year service of the UNEF, the many important actions of the Security Council and the General Assembly, the successive Secretaries-General and other United Nations officials—these are a great and memorable chapter in United Nations history. In the Near East, more than in any other region, the world has looked to the United Nations to keep the door closed on the spectre of war. Now the door has come unhinged. The fact is not a reason to question the motives of the United Nations handling of the matter. Nor is it a reason for despair or handwringing."

Notwithstanding such optimism, he could not even obtain a short ten-minute recess when he requested it for a reason that he considered too "delicate to state." Ambassador Fedorenko of the U.S.S.R. objected strongly. "We do not understand," he said, "the explanation given by the representative of the United States, who suddenly showed some mysterious delicacy concerning the reasons why we should interrupt the work of the Security Council . . . There is absolutely no reason for that kind of staged adjournment . . . It would be reasonable for the members of the Security Council to continue their business-like meeting without any further delay." Goldberg had no choice and yielded: "I find my friend Mr. Fedorenko singularly obtuse. I withdraw my request." And the President added woefully: "I should like to say that the Chair would in normal circumstances give equal consideration to a similar request on the part of any member. But the Chair will not insist on this recess."

The representative of the U.S.S.R. later expressed his opinion "that the Security Council, entrusted by the Charter with primary responsibility for the maintenance of international peace and security, must in present conditions decisively condemn provocations and threats against Arab States." He mentioned that the Soviet delegation had previously "stated its views concerning the so-called initiative of Canada and Denmark in the Security Council. We continue to consider that the appeal of these two NATO countries to the Security Council was part of a campaign artificially inflated by certain circles, a campaign whose true aims have nothing to do with concern for peace and security in the Near East. In the present initiative of Canada and Denmark one can see reflected as in a pool of water the displeasure of those imperialistic circles who quite recently felt themselves to be the masters in the Near East and who stationed their armed forces where they saw fit—but those forces, by dint of the sovereign rights of the States of the Near East, were asked to leave."

Arthur Goldberg and Nikolai Fedorenko subsequently exchanged rhetorical jabs by exercising their "right of reply." In answer to Goldberg's reply, Fedorenko once again resorted to literary references: "Of course, I could use the original language of the great genius, the master of the fable, Krylov, who enriched our literature. But I think that things are quite clear and there is no need to resort to poetic quotations, which I am sure are well known to all those who attended primary school."

Goldberg responded to Fedorenko's answer to his reply: "The United States is opposed to belligerent acts and violence by anyone in the Middle East, no matter what their political ideology or alignment may be. We respect their right to their own political systems and to make their own alignments. We stand ready to endorse the Secretary-General's appeal to all the parties concerned to exercise special restraint, to forego belligerence and to avoid all other actions which could increase tension, to allow the Council to deal with the underlying causes of the present crisis and to seek solutions. Can the Soviet Union say the same?"

Fedorenko reacted at once: "It seems to me the representative of the United States did not listen carefully enough to our statement," he retorted. "We were most clear in setting forth the position of the Soviet Union on this problem, and had he listened with due attention, I doubt that he would have asked any questions such as what he asked of us a few minutes ago." After this introduction, Fedorenko clarified the Soviet position "in this matter" as follows: "The Soviet Union has declared that it is guided by its awareness of high responsibility for the maintenance of peace and security in the Near East and that it condemns the aggressive policy carried on by Tel-Aviv against its Arab neighbours." As for the Secretary-General's appeal for restraint, which was endorsed by the United States and to which Goldberg's question specifically referred, Fedorenko said: "As far as the Secretary-General's report is concerned, that report is before the Security Council and it speaks for itself. Why, I ask, does anyone have to indulge in arbitrary interpretations of that report, interpretations which, in the end, serve only the interests of those who are continuing their acts of aggression?"

So, Goldberg's question was answered by a question. He did not further exercise his right to reply at the same meeting, but waited until the next day, May 30, 1967, when he said: "I shall speak very briefly in exercise of my right to reply, and I shall do so in terms of what I conceive the main function of this Council to be at the present time—that is, not to say anything that might exacerbate a situation which is by common recognition very tense, very grave, very serious and menacing to the cause of world peace and security." After this introduction, Goldberg devoted his remarks mainly to a discussion with the United Arab Republic's representative who "slightly touched his professional pride" when discussing a legal problem. As far as Fedorenko's question was concerned, he said only this: "In exercising the right of reply, I shall not encumber the record with the long-standing position of the United States, which is sustained in the records of both the Security Council and the General Assembly. This is in the interests of the impartial consideration of this particular problem."

The next day, May 31, Goldberg introduced the following draft resolution:

> "*The Security Council,*
>
> *Having considered* the report of the Secretary-General in document S/7906,
>
> *Having heard* the statements of the parties,
>
> *Concerned* at the gravity of the situation in the Middle East,
>
> *Noting* that the Secretary-General has in his report expressed the view that 'a peaceful outcome to the present crisis will depend upon a breathing spell which will allow tension to subside from its present explosive level,' and that he therefore urged 'all the parties concerned to exercise special restraint to forgo belligerence and to avoid all other actions which could increase tension, to allow the Council to deal with the underlying causes of the present crisis and to seek solution,'
>
> 1. Calls on all the parties concerned as a first step to comply with the Secretary-General's appeal,

2. Encourages the immediate pursuit of international diplomacy in the interests of pacifying the situation and seeking reasonable, peaceful and just solutions,

3. Decides to keep this issue under urgent and continuous review so that the Council might determine what further steps it might take in the exercise of its responsibilities for the maintenance of international peace and security."

Goldberg stressed that the draft resolution was an interim measure designed to provide time for more deliberate disposition of the underlying issues without prejudice to the ultimate right and claims of any party. On the role of the Security Council in the conflict he said that "it is charged, in Article 24 of the Charter, with 'primary responsibility for the maintenance of international peace and security.' Let us not forget the reason, which is made expressly clear in the same Article. It is: 'In order to ensure prompt and effective action by the United Nations...' To that end the United States believes that the Council ought to take, step by step, the necessary decisions in this extremely grave and important matter... It is not our intention in offering this interim resolution to attempt in any way to evade or delay the exercise by the Council of its responsibility to seek solutions to the underlying causes of the present crisis. On the contrary, our aim is to gain time and to create a climate in which such solutions can be sought under more favorable conditions."

Goldberg elaborated on the task of the Security Council:

"Indeed, our draft resolution takes into account the fact that the Council has two types of responsibilities. In addition to its responsibility to avert an imminent clash, it has also the responsibility conferred by Chapter VI of the Charter and described in the Secretary-General's words:

'. . . to seek, and eventually to find, reasonable, peaceful and just solutions.' (S/7906, para. 19)

And corresponding responsibility rests also, under the Charter, on every Member State in the international community to support our common effort in the United Nations to achieve peace and security in the Near East.

There is one great issue in the balance here today: the issue of keeping the peace in the Near East, with all that that implies for world security. But we in this Council must also recognize that we face another issue as well: the issue of the potency and efficacy of the United Nations."

At the same meeting Soviet Ambassador Fedorenko answered his United States colleague. "Just now," said Fedorenko, "when the representative of the United States again took the floor to comment on his draft resolution, we heard once more for the tenth time well-known terms such as 'peace-loving,' 'justice,' 'legality,' and so on and so on. These statements remind us of repetitive sermons and, at least in our ears, they have a strange sound indeed. Is it not ironic that the official representatives of the United States of America strive to present Washington in the role of advocate of peace, defender of justice and legality, even on a world scale? Hearing such statements, does the question not come to mind: How can these arguments of the United States representative concerning high-sounding principles of international law be reconciled with the deeds, with the practical acts of Washington? In what way are the statements of the United States Ambassador Arthur Goldberg in keeping with the most flagrant violations by the United States of the most elementary principles of international law? And he is a very well-known jurist, so that this especially concerns his own field..."

Goldberg immediately responded to the charge that he had issued "repetitive sermons" by alluding to the "Chinese proverbs" of his Soviet colleague. "The representative of the Soviet Union," said Goldberg," has given this Council a disquisition on international law—not only on this situation, but on other situations—and he has asked me to answer his legal commentary. I am glad to oblige, and this is my answer. On legal questions, the Soviet representative speaks like the great authority on Chinese literature that indeed he is. I shall leave it to him to rely on Chinese proverbs, and I shall continue to rely on international law, including treaties to which his Government is a party. Ambassador Fedorenko also complains that I have repeatedly used words such as 'peace-loving,' justice' and 'legality.' I should not imagine that it would be necessary in this Council to apologize for using these words, and I regret that I have to serve notice on him that I shall use them again and again until they are heeded... I am not surprised, however, that the words 'peace-loving,' 'justice' and 'legality' have a strange sound to Ambassador Fedorenko. I am just surprised that he admits this so frankly and so publicly."

Without delay Fedorenko repaid in kind. "We have just heard," he said, " a dissertation from the representative of the United States, who, as was to be expected, will continue his exercise in legal terminology and eloquence and, as an experienced lawyer, will evade any answer with regard to the substance of the matter." He then returned to his favorite proverbs and noted that they were not of Chinese origin. "We would like to hear from our respected colleague," said Fedorenko in his reply, "who is often called 'Justice', how he judges these statements made in Washington and the practical deeds

THE WAR IN THE MIDDLE EAST 1967

which in the most clear-cut manner refute these statements and which are in blatant contradiction with the sound of these statements made by the official circles of the United States. This is just as much a mockery in Russian, in English or in Chinese—and even in Japanese, since I used some Japanese proverbs recently; they were Japanese proverbs, and nothing else, but for some reason the United States representative thought otherwise. It may be that everything sounds the same to the United States representative, that any Eastern wisdom sounds the same, that any Eastern folklore is the same, that everything is monotonous if it is not something in his own language. But there are various cultures, great cultures, and there is different popular wisdom in various parts of the world. It is because the peoples of the world judge on the basis of general wisdom that we asked this question of our respected colleague from the United States: how do you explain, not your declarations, but your actions, the actions of the United States Government especially as far as the blockade is concerned, a blockade against a full-fledged Member of the United Nations? . . ."

Goldberg answered briefly: "I said the other day, and I repeat it now, that at any time when the representative of the Soviet Union is prepared, with respect to an item properly on the agenda, to talk about the matter and to vote on it, I am ready to do so, whether it concerns Vietnam, Cuba or anything else. The chips are down not only when you make speeches but when you vote: I have found that when we try to inscribe items so that we can discuss these important issues there are objections. Let the objections be withdrawn and we shall proceed to discuss these subjects at the proper time. We are discussing the item on our agenda now."

The final word in this Security Council dialogue of May

WAR ON WAR

31, 1967 belonged to the representative of the Soviet Union: "We are convinced that once again our colleague of the United States is avoiding a clear-cut answer to the question we have asked him. . . It is not a question of what is or is not written on a piece of paper; this question is inscribed on the agenda of life itself, and it has not been withdrawn. And life is implacable in this regard. There is no justification for this kind of arbitrary behaviour, especially on the part of a great State, a permanent member of the Security Council. It ill behooves anyone, especially a Justice, to avoid answering this question."

* * *

Preparations for the war in the Middle East were in full swing when the Security Council met again on June 3, 1967. None of the members, of course, realized that only hours remained for action to avoid the outbreak of war. Hans Tabor of Denmark, who had taken over the Presidency for the month of June, began by announcing that he wished to correct an error in the United States draft resolution "which had crept into the final paragraph of the preamble, namely, the omission of a comma in the second quotation from the report of the Secretary-General."

After this announcement, he gave the floor to Gideon Rafael, the representative of Israel, who stated that "the crisis in the Middle East erupted without warning on 16 May when an Egyptian general sent an ultimatum to the commander of UNEF. At the same time as he asked for the removal of the United Nations force, he moved his own forces into the positions held by the United Nations." Rafael complained that for the previous twelve days, since the Canadian-Danish initiative urgently convening the Security Council, the Council had

THE WAR IN THE MIDDLE EAST 1967

debated the matter, "at the same time one Arab spokesman after another has come to this table not to alleviate the dangerous tensions, but to fan the flames of violence and hatred."

He quoted Emperor Haile Selassie of Ethiopia, who had declared, in 1936, before Mussolini's attack on his country, "that it was not the Covenant of the League [of Nations] that was at stake, but international morality." He also quoted Adlai L. Stevenson who had once said in the Security Council: "Were we to do nothing until the knife was sharpened? Were we to stand idly by until it was at our throats?" The representative of Syria, Daoudy, later spoke, accusing Rafael of "distorting the facts" by pretending "that the present crisis in the Middle East erupted on May 16, 1967" (when the United Nations Emergency Force was asked by the United Arab Republic to leave its positions). According to Daoudy, the crisis started on November 29, 1947, when the partition of Palestine was enforced. After the intervention of other Arab representatives (from Morocco and Saudi Arabia), the customary Goldberg-Fedorenko dialogue was resumed. Fedorenko began by saying:

> "The Soviet delegation has already had occasion to note that the representative of the United States at this table has often, in the Security Council, indulged in lengthy discourse on the question of international navigation, on principles of international law, on legal principles and provisions, and so on, and it seems that nothing can make him lose countenance. Nothing has prevented him from depicting, in all the colours of the rainbow, the policy of the United States of America as an advocate of the principle of free international navigation, as a defender of legality, of justice. He has shown in words great concern for this principle all over the world.

WAR ON WAR

We have already drawn the attention of the Council to the fact that these hypocritical statements, far from being in accordance with reality, are quite obviously flagrantly at variance with deeds, with the criminal practices of the United States of America."

After he adverted to "pharisaic preachings" concerning "love for peace, for justice and for international law," Goldberg felt "impelled to exercise his right of reply." He explained the American policy of 1962 concerning the Cuban missile crisis. He then made the observation that "the primary function of this Council, if it is to harmonize the actions of nations, is to observe elementary diplomatic courtesy and usage." In accordance with such usage, it was appropriate to discuss only statements by representatives of the United States Government in the Security Council; unfortunately, he said, some representatives expressed opinions regarding the exercise by private citizens of their convictions. In answer, Fedorenko suggested that it might "be more reasonable for our colleague from the United States, instead of lecturing others, to recommend to his Government that it cease this risky, adventurous nuclear game which, as we know, is still going on." He quoted a warning by the Secretary-General of the United Nations to the effect that "the world is now in the first stage of the third world war." Referring to the attack on the Soviet vessel *Turkestan* (on which Goldberg had promised to provide a report, upon investigation, through normal diplomatic channels), Fedorenko said: "It may be that this crime was not committed by the United States Air Force but by people from Mars or by dark forces landed from planets in outer space. Or is it that our United States colleague will tell us that it is necessary to create special committees of investigation—congressional committees perhaps?"

THE WAR IN THE MIDDLE EAST 1967

Goldberg retorted:

"If we needed any proof that the Soviet Union's conception of helping to relieve tension in the present crisis is to engage in a cold-war exercise, we have just heard it. The United States' conception is otherwise. We shall continue in this situation to exercise our influence to help keep the peace in the Near East."

The meeting adjourned without any decision. The President of the Council, Hans Tabor of Denmark, announced that the next meeting would be held on Monday, June 5, 1967 at 3 p.m. "on the understanding that members of the Council will hold themselves available for consultations also over the week-end and for an urgent meeting of the Council before Monday afternoon in case there are any new developments that may require the convening of the Council."

He was right in anticipating the possibility of new developments. It was on account of these developments that the Security Council met on Monday, June 5, not at three o'clock in the afternoon, but at nine thirty that morning.

* * *

After opening the June 5 session the President informed the Council that he had received, at 3:10 that morning, an official communication from the Representative of Israel and at 3:30 an official communication from the Representative of the United Arab Republic informing him that war had broken out between the two countries. The Israeli Representative stated that Egyptian land and air forces had moved against Israel, while the U.A.R. Representative accused Israel of aggression against his country.

WAR ON WAR

The President of the Security Council then announced that the Secretary-General had confirmed that exchanges of fire and air activity had been going on in the area since the early hours of the morning. He gave the floor to Secretary-General U Thant, who stated that "the United Nations sources have no means of ascertaining how the hostilities were initiated. As usual, reports coming from the parties are conflicting, but all agree that serious military action on land and in the air is taking place at a number of points and is spreading."

The Secretary-General further said that "as far as information from UNEF is concerned, it must be remembered that UNEF is no longer on the Line, but is concentrated in its camps and is in the process of withdrawal." He quoted a report from General Rikhye, Commander of UNEF, "much of which has been given by the U.A.R. liaison service in Gaza." According to this report, "at 0800 hours local time today two Israel aircraft violated U.A.R. airspace over Gaza town." The report mentioned the outbreak of other hostilities, among them an Israeli air raid on Cairo which was denied by Israeli authorities. General Odd Bull also informed U Thant that "firing in Jerusalem commenced at 1125 hours local time and was continuing." At 1145 hours local time Jordan and Israel informed General Bull that they accepted his request for a cease-fire at 1200 hours local time. (This would mean that a cease-fire had been accepted as early as 20 minutes after the fighting had broken out). The report added: "Since sporadic mortar firing from Jordan continued after the cease-fire, a second cease-fire was proposed for 1230 hours local time and accepted by both sides." (Obviously, Jordan and Israel were at peace.) A more difficult situation developed, according to the Secretary-General, on the Israel-Syria Armistice Demarcation Line, where air battles were reported. "The Senior Israel

THE WAR IN THE MIDDLE EAST 1967

Delegate to the Israel-Syria Mixed Armistice Commission informed the UNTSO officer in charge at Tiberias at 1218 hours local time that Israel considered itself in a state of war with Syria."

The report of the Secretary-General mentioned that Government House in the Jordanian sector of Jerusalem, where the United Nations forces had their headquarters, had been occupied by Jordanian troops. The Secretary-General considered this to be a breach of extreme seriousness and therefore sent the following telegram to King Hussein:

> "His Majesty King Hussein, Hashemite Kingdom of Jordan, Amman, Jordan.
>
> Your Majesty, I have just been advised at 0900 hours local time that all communications with Government House have ended because of its occupation by Jordanian troops. This is a breach of extreme seriousness. I appeal to Your Majesty with utmost urgency to order the immediate removal of Jordanian troops from the grounds and buildings of the Government House compound in Jerusalem. As Your Majesty knows, this compound has been respected by both parties to the Hashemite Kingdom of Jordan-Israel Mixed Armistice Commission as the Headquarters of the United Nations Truce Supervision Organization and therefore under the exclusive United Nations occupation and control.
>
> U Thant, Secretary-General
> of the United Nations"

The Secretary-General also notified the Security Council that "at 1245 hours local time Israel artillery opened fire on two camps of the Indian Contingent of UNEF which were in process of being abandoned, and soon thereafter U.A.R. tanks

WAR ON WAR

surrounded one of the camps which still contained one reduced Indian company." A UNEF convoy on the road between Gaza and Rafah was strafed by an Israeli aircraft on the morning of June 5, 1967 and three Indian soldiers were killed.

This information caused the representative of India, Gopalaswami Parthasarathi, to "condemn this Israeli action and protest most vigorously against it." He described it as a "wanton, irresponsible and brutal action by the ruling circles in Israel." The President of the Council then gave the floor to the representatives of the two parties. Gideon Rafael of Israel stated that "in the early hours of this morning Egyptian armoured columns moved in an offensive thrust against Israel's borders. At the same time Egyptian planes took off from airfields in Sinai and struck out towards Israel." He quoted the order of the day of the Egyptian commander, General Murtagi, of June 3, 1967, in which he had said that "the outcome of this special moment is of historic importance for our Arab people and its holy war for restoring the rights of the Arabs which were plundered from them in Palestine." The representative of the United Arab Republic, Mohamed Awad El Kony, stated that the Israelis were the aggressors. "The dimensions of the Israeli attack are so wide," said El Kony, "that no one can doubt the premeditated nature of this aggression. Israelis are attacking, all of a sudden and simultaneously, the Gaza strip, Sinai, Cairo airports, and Sharm El Sheikh, together with other places."

Undoubtedly, a major war had broken out in the Middle East. The Security Council adjourned "for urgent consultations."

* * *

THE WAR IN THE MIDDLE EAST 1967

The next day, June 6, 1967, at 6:30 p.m., the President of the Council called the meeting to order, announcing that the consultations had resulted in a unanimous agreement on a draft resolution calling for an immediate cease-fire. The resolution was adopted unanimously, without debate. It read:

> *"The Security Council,*
> *Noting* the oral report of the Secretary-General in this situation,
> *Having heard* the statements made in the Council,
> *Concerned* at the outbreak of fighting and with the menacing situation in the Near East,
> 1. Calls upon the Governments concerned as a first step to take forthwith all measures for an immediate cease-fire and for a cessation of all military activities in the area,
> 2. Requests the Secretary-General to keep the Council promptly and currently informed on the situation."

After the adoption of the resolution, the representatives of the United States, Ethiopia, France, United Kingdom, the Soviet Union, Argentina, Canada, Brazil, Japan, Bulgaria, Mali, China, India, and Denmark each explained their votes. Hans Tabor of Denmark—the President of the Council—then expressed the "happiness" of his Government "that it has now proved possible as a first step to adopt unanimously a resolution calling for a cease-fire." He said further that "the whole world has been waiting for this call."

Subsequently, the representatives of Iraq, Israel, Syrian Arab Republic and Morocco made lengthy statements. At the end of the meeting, during which several interventions in the exercise of the right of reply were heard, Soviet Ambassador Fedorenko asked for an immediate enforcement of the Security Council decision. The President gave assurance that the necessary measures and steps would be taken "in order to see that, on our side, everything is done in order that the parties will comply with this decision."

However, the fighting did not stop. The next morning, June 7, 1967, Ambassador Fedorenko requested an urgent meeting of the Security Council, which was convened at 1 p.m. The Soviet representative submitted a draft resolution which, in its preamble, stated that in spite of the Security Council's appeal for a cessation of all military activities in the Near East, "military activities in the area are continuing." The resolution demanded "that the Governments concerned should as a first step cease fire and discontinue all military activities at 2000 hours GMT on 7 June 1967."

The Secretary-General informed the Council that he had received a telegram from the Foreign Minister of Jordan accepting the cease-fire. The representative of Brazil, on a point of order, thereupon suggested a twenty-minute recess. The representative of the United States did not object but stated:

> "My delegation has been conscious of the gravity of this situation not since last night, but for three weeks. At the meeting of the Council last night I made specific references to the records of this Council and official statements on behalf of our Government.
>
> I think that the sequence of events should be very clear to the members of this Council and to the world community. We pointed out the extreme gravity of the situation. If certain Powers had not objected and had not deprecated our statements about the gravity of the situation, a resolution would have been in the hands of the Council for effective action to avert the outbreak of the hostilities in the Near East, with all the consequences that have ensued. But regrettably, our con-

sistent requests and our consistent demands, for action by this Council to call on all parties, in the strongest terms possible, to exercise restraint were not heeded."

The representative of the Soviet Union did not object to a recess. However, he expressed his opinion that, according to the rules of procedure of the Security Council, a motion for suspension or adjournment of a meeting should be decided "without debate." He noted that "we have in fact opened the debate:"

> "I am thinking of the rather lengthy statement—given the hour—made by the representative of the United States. We would like to repeat again that this is no time for debates, for reminiscences, and even less for quoting one's own speeches, whatever pleasure that may afford to the author."

The meeting was then adjourned for fifteen minutes. It was not resumed until somewhat more than fifteen minutes had elapsed. This delay drew the following statement at the beginning of the resumed meeting by the Soviet representative:

> "We are compelled to take the floor to speak on a point of order. First of all, we should like to draw attention to the fact that the decision taken by the Security Council is not being precisely carried out. A decision was taken to suspend or adjourn the meeting until 2 p.m. Our work was resumed at 2:30 p.m. This cannot be considered normal."

The President expressed his regret for the delay and added:

> "However, the day before yesterday we decided to have a

short recess for consultations, and that short recess lasted for eleven hours."

The draft resolution submitted by the USSR was finally adopted unanimously. Canada submitted a resolution requesting the President of the Security Council, with the assistance of the Secretary-General, "to take the necessary measures to bring about full and effective compliance" with the resolutions of the Council. Before this resolution could even be discussed, the Soviet representative asked for its distribution "in the usual fashion" to the members of the Council. In the meantime, the representatives of the United Arab Republic and Israel made statements which were followed by interventions by several representatives in the exercise of their rights of reply. The Soviet representative also made a statement in which he once again alluded to Oriental wisdom. He said:

> "The representative of the United States in his numerous statements yesterday and today, making marathon speeches concerning Washington's peaceful intentions, creates a kind of screen behind which at the same time and punctuated with this verbal accompaniment, the aggressive forces of Israel, disregarding decisions of the Security Council immediately to cease its military invasion, continues to violate the sovereignty of the Arab States. By fire and sword they take Arab territory—the territory of their Arab neighbours—and by armed force carry out their plans of conquest.
> Closely following speeches and deeds, we should like to remind those to whom this is addressed of a very characteristic and interesting observation: 'Do not bring false sacrifices to the true Buddha.' "

He read to the Council an official statement which had

THE WAR IN THE MIDDLE EAST 1967

been issued by the Soviet Government that very same day. In it Israel was warned that "if the Israeli Government now does not immediately fulfil the common demand of States for an immediate cease-fire, which is expressed in the Security Council's resolution, the Soviet Union will revise its attitude in respect of Israel and adopt a decision concerning the further maintenance of diplomatic relations with Israel."

The Secretary-General then read a communication from the Permanent Representative of Israel quoting a statement by Israel's Foreign Minister in the Security Council on June 6, 1967, immediately following the adoption of the cease-fire resolution. The latter had said that "Israel welcomes the appeal for the cease-fire . . . But . . . the implementation depends on the absolute and sincere acceptance and co-operation of the other parties."

The Security Council, after protracted debate on the question whether to suspend the meeting for fifteen minutes, for half an hour, until some time later in the evening, or *sine die,* finally agreed to adjourn "until such time as we can vote on the (Canadian) draft resolution."

In the meantime armed hostilities were raging on all fronts.

* * *

The next day, June 8, 1967, it was the turn of the United States to request an urgent meeting of the Security Council.

In opening the meeting at 2:50 p.m., President Tabor announced that at 10:40 that morning he had received a request from the Permanent Representative of the United States for an urgent meeting "because the fighting, in spite of the call from the Security Council, was continuing in the area."

WAR ON WAR

He said that "later, the representative of the USSR also requested an emergency meeting."

The Secretary-General first read the following message from the Foreign Minister of Kuwait:

> "Gratefully received your cable concerning resolutions of Security Council for cease-fire. I am sorry to inform you that the Government of Kuwait will not observe nor adhere to these resolutions which do not condemn Israeli aggressors. The resolutions also ignored the just rights of the Palestinians in their homeland. With highest considerations."

The Council was also advised of a telegram sent by the Foreign Minister of Israel on June 7, 1967, informing the President of the Security Council that at 4:45 p.m. New York time, he had advised the Secretary-General that the Israeli Government had accepted the Security Council's call for an immediate cease-fire, provided that the other parties similarly accepted. U Thant also announced that the Foreign Minister of Jordan had informed him in a further cable of June 7 of his Government's immediate acceptance of the ceaee-fire resolution.

The U.S. representative introduced a draft resolution which noted the acceptance of the cease-fire by Israel and Jordan and stated that the Security Council "insists that all the other parties concerned immediately comply with the Council's repeated demands for a cease-fire." It also called "for discussions promptly thereafter among the parties concerned, using such third party or United Nations assistance as they may wish, looking toward the establishment of viable arrangements encompassing the withdrawal and disengagement of armed personnel."

THE WAR IN THE MIDDLE EAST 1967

In his lengthy statement, Ambassador Goldberg reaffirmed the wish of his government that all the nations and peoples of the Middle East might reach a true peace "of justice, mutual tolerance and creative growth." He said that "a wise philosopher once observed that there is no conflict which cannot be resolved if it is dealt with at a higher level than that on which it occurred."

After this statement, U Thant read a letter from the Permanent Representative of the United Arab Republic, dated June 8, 1967, to the effect that his Government had decided to accept the cease-fire, "on the condition that the other party ceases fire."

The Soviet Ambassador then presented a draft resolution which read as follows:

"The Security Council,
Noting that Israel has disregarded the Security Council decisions calling for the cessation of military activities (S/RES/233 of 6 June 1967 and S/RES/234 of 7 June 1967),

Considering that Israel not only has not halted military activities but has made use of the time elapsed since the adoption of the aforementioned Council resolutions in order to seize additional territory of the United Arab Republic and Jordan,

Noting that even now Israel is continuing military activities instead of halting its aggression, thus defying the United Nations and all peace-loving States,

1. *Vigorously condemns* Israel's aggressive activities and its violations of the aforementioned Security Council resolutions, of the United Nations Charter and of United Nations principles,

2. *Demands* that Israel should immediately halt its military

activities against neighbouring Arab states and should remove all its troops from the territory of those States and withdraw them behind the armistice lines."

Lord Caradon of the United Kingdom stated that the Security Council should have acted twenty-four hours earlier. "Nevertheless," he said further, "we took the essential first step together, and I pay my respectful tribute to all those, including the representative of the Soviet Union, who contributed to making that result possible." He obviously believed that, with the acceptance of the cease-fire by the three belligerents, the war would be at an end. Lord Caradon felt that the time had come to praise the United Nations:

> "There have been those who have been quick to declare the failure of the United Nations. Those who have sought to denigrate international effort rejoiced. There were some —who have never been ready to strengthen the international Organization while there was time and opportunity to do so—who were ready to pronounce its impotence. There were those who were prepared to see the efforts of the past twenty-one years to establish international co-operation and international authority destroyed and betrayed. Others may be so prepared; we cannot be."

He added:

> "We now have the opportunity to prove such people wrong. We now have an opportunity to show that there is nothing wrong with an organization which includes great nations and middle-sized nations and small nations and rich and poor nations alike. We now have an opportunity to prove that there is nothing wrong with the principle that every nation has a right to be heard, but no nation has a right to

dominate. We still have an opportunity to show that there is nothing wrong with the Charter or the Organization, but with those who refuse to use it. The events of this week have themselves emphasized the necessity of using it."

The optimism of the British Ambassador with regard to the role of the United Nations in the Middle East crisis was challenged by Israel's Foreign Minister, Abba Eban, who spoke after him. "The emphasis in Israel's thinking," said Eban, "is not so much on the authority of international bodies but on the sovereign responsibility of the Governments concerned, by direct and bilateral contact, to work out the conditions and the elements of their coexistence."

His speech was characterized by Soviet Ambassador Fedorenko as "reminiscent of the lecturings of an elementary school teacher." "If the Minister had a great store of wisdom at his command," the Soviet representative said, "he might render yeoman service to the Government of Tel-Aviv, because that is what the Government needs most of all." This exchange typified the atmosphere of the Security Council after three States engaged in war had declared that they were accepting a cease-fire.

* * *

At one o'clock on the morning of June 9, 1967, the President of the Security Council was officially informed that the Government of Syria had also accepted the appeal of the Council for a cease-fire.

However, at 5:30 that same morning, the representative of Israel informed the President of the Security Council that "Syrian artillery fire continued to be directed against Israel villages for many hours after this message was received by the United Nations."

At 6 o'clock in the morning the President received a request from the Permanent Representative of Syria for an urgent meeting of the Security Council. He convened the meeting at 12:30 p.m.

The Secretary-General spoke first and read several messages confirming that the war had continued. The representative of Syria bitterly charged Israel with the blame and the Israeli representative did the same for Syria. The President submitted a resolution demanding that hostilities cease forthwith. The resolution was adopted unanimously. Ambassador Goldberg then said he had been prepared to vote for a ceasefire before 10 o'clock in the morning; unfortunately, over two hours had been lost before the Council was able to come to this decision. Concerning the reason for the delay, the United States Ambassador said:

> "This delay was no fault of yours, Mr. President. Throughout your handling of this grave affair, you have acted with extreme expedition and have made every effort to ensure that the Council would act urgently and energetically in the interest of stopping the fighting and bringing about more stable conditions in the area.
>
> I would be less than candid if I did not also say that the delay was not due to the parties involved. Both parties involved were ready for us to proceed at 10 a.m. Now, what is the delay due to? It is, in my opinion, more than time to call a spade a spade. The delay is due to the fact that other members of the Council insist upon attempting to inject into our discussions matter which should be handled next. It is because some members of the Council do not adequately, in my view, understand the extreme urgency of bringing the fighting to an end and because they inject into our discussion

matters, important matters, which should and will require the Council's consideration after we bring the fighting to an end."*

Goldberg's accusation was not restricted to the two-hour delay on June 9. "The same sort of unfortunate delay took place on Monday and Tuesday," the United States representative went on. He also recalled the delay on May 24, 1967. "If all members of the Council had been prepared on 24 May to support the resolution that you, Mr. President, offered on behalf of your country, joined by the representative of Canada, perhaps no conflict would have taken place." He then criticized the United Nations:

> "Part of our problem here has been the fact that some members of this Council have not been willing to authorize the appropriate officials of the United Nations to take action in implementation of the Council's resolutions. It is not a high-mark in the history of this Organization that a simple draft resolution offered a few days ago by the representative of Canada was not promptly acted upon but was thought to be something that required study and consideration. What kind of study, what kind of consideration, when what was called for was all the energies and resources of this Organization in the interest of bringing the fighting to an end so that the Council could then proceed to deal with the underlying causes of the conflict, to pacify the situation and to help bring about a durable peace . . .

---

* It is worthwhile to note that the statement and charges made by Ambassador Goldberg are completely omitted in the Report of the Security Council to the General Assembly (Official Records, 22nd Session, Supplement No. 2, A/6702), pp. 42-43, where the meeting of June 9 was reported. It is, of course, included in the Verbatim Record of the meeting (S/PV. 1352), pp. 23-25.

WAR ON WAR

We are not doing credit to the United Nations by the manner in which we have been proceeding . . .

If we go back, as we shall have to go back at the appropriate time, and consider what happened in this situation, we shall see that it has been a lack of ability to concert our actions here so that conflict may be avoided; and also a lack of ability to concert our actions here once conflict has broken out, to stop the fighting so that there can then be a sorting-out of the problems that develop whenever fighting takes place . . .

Because of our delay, people have lost their lives. That is something for which we have to assume the responsibility before the conscience of the world.

Ambassador Fedorenko responded immediately. He sharply condemned Israel and then turned to the United States:

"Whom is the representative of the United States trying to hypnotize? The Security Council perchance? Is it not symptomatic that the representative of the United States in the Security Council speaks of all things except the fact that Israel has committed aggression and that Israel has seized by force the lands of Arabs in violation of all principles of international law and of the provisions of the Charter?"

The representative of India, Parthasarathi, complained bitterly over the fact that the resolutions of the Security Council had remained ineffective. "It is over sixty hours since we adopted Resolution 233 asking for an immediate cease-fire in the Middle East. It is nearly forty hours since the second resolution, Resolution 234, was passed by the Council and the time-limit imposed by the Council expired. It is almost eighteen hours ago that we heard the Secretary-General make the welcome announcement that the Government of the United

THE WAR IN THE MIDDLE EAST 1967

Arab Republic had accepted the cease-fire. Last night, Syria made a similar announcement." Parthasarathi asked: "Why is it that despite assurances that the aggressor will stop its predatory moves and cease further action, the cease-fire has not become fully effective in the Middle East?"

The resolution adopted by the Council called for the Secretary-General to report within two hours about the compliance of Israel and Syria with the demand that hostilities cease forthwith. The resolution was adopted at the beginning of the meeting, at approximately 1:30 p.m. The debate lasted until 4:30 p.m., when the meeting recessed with an announcement by the President that the Council would meet again at 6:30 p.m.

* * *

The Security Council's next meeting was called to order at 7:15. The Soviet representative, speaking on a point of order, asked for the grounds for the delay. The President replied that it was due to the fact that one of the members had wanted to talk with the head of his Government; the President had also engaged in consultations with the members, including the representative of the Soviet Union. Ambassador Fedorenko then stated that "it was not you who consulted with me, but it was I who went to you to protest against the delay in beginning the meeting of the Security Council at the precise time when hostilities were taking place, when people were dying, when towns were being destroyed." The President confirmed that fact, adding that, after he had received the protest, he had discussed another question with the representative of the Soviet Union.

The Secretary-General reported that hostilities were still going on. Accusations and counter-accusations were made by the representatives of Syria and Israel. Following a discussion, the President stated that there seemed to be agreement among all members that the Security Council should request the parties concerned to extend all possible co-operation to United Nations observers in the discharge of their responsibilities. Through these observers the Council expected to be informed whether peace has been restored.

Lord Caradon of the United Kingdom said that he should be anxious "to stay here through the night if necessary." He assured the Council that he "should even be happy to listen to any given number of speeches from the representative of the Soviet Union" because he "can think of no pleasanter way of spending the night." But "it does us no good and it does not advance our purpose to listen to accusations and counter-accusations."

Ambassador Fedorenko then said:

> "I cannot refrain from expressing my admiration for the presence of mind and real British humour which was demonstrated by our British colleague. He has, of course, expressed a very attractive idea about how we can spend tonight. But I have certain doubts about it. He probably forgot my proletarian background which, I fear, is not quite consonant with such high society as the company of a British Lord, even a socialist Lord."

The meeting was adjourned at 10:50 p.m. with the understanding that all members would hold themselves available for an urgent meeting at any time, should the Council be faced with an emergency situation. At 2 o'clock on the morning of June 10, the President of the Council received a request for an emergency meeting from a representative of the Syrian Government. The meeting was convened at 4:30 a.m.

THE WAR IN THE MIDDLE EAST 1967

The Secretary-General reported "continuing hostilities in the area east of Lake Tiberias in Syria and the eastern bank of the Jordan River" and that Damascus Airport and suburbs had been bombed by the Israel air forces. The Israel Foreign Office had denied the air attack on Damascus or its airport, asserting that Israel aircraft were over Syria only to provide protective cover for Israel forces.

In an atmosphere of extreme uneasiness, the Security Council spent several hours of the early morning of June 10 trying to determine whether Damascus had been bombed or not. Ambassador Fedorenko used unprecedented language with reference to the Israeli Ambassador:

> "Gideon Rafael sat here five hours among us and openly misled the Council to divert the attention of the Security Council and play for time, for the annexationist purposes of the Israeli hordes, for the accomplishment by the leaders in Tel Aviv of a new crime against peaceful people. That was a deliberate misleading of the Council. But this outrageous lie is now exposed. And we ask: How can we tolerate here in this lofty organ this monstrous cynicism and deliberate falsification? Can this go on with impunity? After all this, has the representative of Tel Aviv any right to sit any longer in the Security Council?"

Ambassador Rafael tried to make a point of order but did not succeed. He spoke only after Fedorenko had finished his statement in which he appealed "to take urgent and decisive measures to call a halt to the aggressor" and assured that "the full weight of responsibility for the consequences will rest on the shoulders of those members of the Council who hinder the adoption of necessary measures."

Mr. Rafael said:

WAR ON WAR

"I wish to be advised by the President, in the first instance, whether it is permitted to engage in personal abuse directed at representatives acting here on behalf of their Governments. I can take this abuse, but I wonder whether it fits the dignity of this Council."

After statements by the representatives of the United States (Mr. Goldberg) and Bulgaria (Mr. Tarabanov), Ambassador Fedorenko took the American representative to task. He stressed that the Secretary-General's report on the bombing of Damascus originated with General Bull, and asked:

"Is that source sufficiently authorized and authentic? We should like to ask: Where is your impartiality, distinguished Justice? Why have you lost the gift of speech and completely disregarded this fact?"

The tension mounted with each new report that arrived. The meeting was adjourned at 6 a.m. in order to give the members a chance to consider the reports. It was resumed at 6:25. Ambassador Rafael categorically denied that any Israeli aircraft had attacked Damascus. The Secretary-General, however, stated that General Bull had again reported that "bombing and hostilities continue along the eastern ridges of Lake Tiberias shores in Syria, as well as on the eastern bank of Jordan river, north of Lake Tiberias, and that Damascus has been bombed by Israel air force." Ambassador Tarabanov then delivered a long speech asking for "condemnation of the aggression and the withdrawal of troops to their original positions." The Secretary-General finally informed the Council that he had received a new report from General Bull. The Israeli Foreign Office had informed Bull that there had been no air attack on the city of Damascus. The representative of France moved for

THE WAR IN THE MIDDLE EAST 1967

the adjournment of the meeting until 7:30, because the representatives needed time to read and to study the reports, and not only to listen to them.

A new meeting of the Security Council was convened at 8:10 a.m. A good portion of it was spent on a procedural matter: whether the President should transmit a question posed by a member of the Council to a representative present at the meeting. The rest of this second morning meeting of Saturday, June 10, 1967, was devoted to an angry exchange of accusations between various representatives, the comments of one being characterized by another as being "in violation of every type of diplomatic usage," "beneath contempt," "and I would not even purport to dignify them with an answer."

It was not the last meeting of the Security Council on June 10. At 9:15 in the evening the Security Council met for the third time at the urgent request of the Soviet representative. Ambassador Fedorenko, in extremely violent language, again denounced the Israeli Government whom he called the "pirates of Tel Aviv." He alleged that "soon after the Security Council adjourned this morning, the capital of the Syrian Arab Republic, Damascus, was subjected to a new attack by the Israeli air force. The city was bombed again by the pirates of Tel Aviv. Moreover, according to accurate and confirmed information, there still was fighting in the region of Kuneitra, fifty-five kilometres from the capital of Syria." Fedorenko stressed "with indignation the inadmissibility of a situation in which the Security Council is being dragged into a shameful farce." He tried to present the case as a conflict of Israel versus the Security Council:

> "What do the so-called representatives of Tel Aviv think the Security Council is? When will they put an end to these

lies and to this deceit? Is this not a confirmation of the assessment of the activities of the Israeli Government which was given by the Soviet delegation at the last meeting of the Security Council, when we said that Israel is deliberately deluding the Security Council?

It is most regrettable, and certainly it is to be condemned, that there are great protectors of the lying representatives of Tel Aviv, and they are sitting at our table here. The Council cannot be associated with the maniacs of the war who cannot with open eyes see the light but can only see through a black patch.

The new facts, the new aggressive and criminal actions of Israel, confirm the view that the Security Council has no further grounds to have any more trust or confidence in Tel Aviv. The action of Israel towards the Arab countries, and the continuing violation by Israel of the decisions of the Security Council, are nothing other than open mockery. The principles of international law are being derided, as is the Organization of the United Nations. It is a mockery of the Security Council and of its decisions. We are saying this in order that no one should harbour any doubts, that no one should harbour any delusions. We understand what is happening here and what attempts are being made to change the whole direction of the work of the Security Council."

Ambassador Fedorenko did not explain further in what direction the work of the Security Council should move. He elaborated only on the policies of Israel and said that "the leaders of Israel are following the shameful practices of the Nazi criminals."

In the ensuing discussion, Ambassador Goldberg of the U.S. clarified his Government's position. "The Security Council should have a single goal, to quench the flames of war in

THE WAR IN THE MIDDLE EAST 1967

the Near East and to begin to move towards peace in the area. Throughout our deliberation on this subject we have attempted by all the means at our disposal to expedite the action of this Council and the action of the United Nations in this direction." He complained that "instead of that, much of the time of this Council is devoted to diatribes against my country about alleged involvement in this conflict." He stated that "the United States is in no way involved in this conflict, but, on the contrary, has used its influence here and diplomatically in the interests of, first, avoiding the conflict, and then bringing it to an end."

A draft resolution was submitted by the U.S. representative calling on the Governments concerned "to issue categoric instructions to all military forces to cease all firing and military activities." In the same draft resolution "any and all violations of the cease-fire" were condemned and a demand was expressed "that the parties scrupulously respect" the cease-fire appeals of the Security Council.

Later at the same meeting, Mr. Fedorenko commented on Mr. Goldberg's speech:

> "The representative of the United States, who, as we could all hear, has just spoken in an extremely pedantic and thoroughly stereotyped fashion, once again has got off a somewhat threadbare tirade about the benevolent policies of Washington which, in the fervid imagination of the speaker, appear to him to emanate an aura of love and general peace. And that, let us note, without even a shadow of reproach with reference to the monstrous aggression in the Middle East and the barbarous war being waged by American imperialism in Vietnam.
>
> Having draped himself in this mythological cloak, the American diplomat went through his pompous monologue,

obviously addressing the television cameras and the audience we know is out there."

He questioned Mr. Goldberg:

"Does he condemn the bombing of Damascus? Does he condemn the fact that the representative of Israel has been cynically misleading the Security Council, denying the seizure of Kuneitra at a time when the town was already in the hands of the Israeli military?"

Mr. Goldberg answered:

"I am prepared, as the draft resolution which I have submitted shows, to condemn all violations of the cease-fire confirmed by the Secretary-General in his report.

I should like to ask a question of the representative of the Soviet Union. Is he prepared to condemn all the violations of the cease-fire confirmed by the Secretary-General in his report?"

Mr. Fedorenko's reply was:

"We have just been convinced again that the American representative has no wish whatsoever to state the truth. As always, when there is a sharp curve, he is trying very risky zigzagging, and instead of a reply he thought of nothing better than to put a question."

The Soviet representative sharply attacked the draft resolution submitted by the United States "which has one objective, which is certainly of bad intent, namely to tender service to the Israeli aggressor, to assist the Israeli aggressor in legalizing, so to speak, and legitimizing the occupation of the territory of Arab countries achieved by violence." He

THE WAR IN THE MIDDLE EAST 1967

expressed the hope that "the representative of the United States will refrain from further maneouvres and will not repeat that this is not a camel but a horse—a horse, a hunchbacked horse."

The tension mounted to the point that the good faith of the President of the Council was challenged when he gave the floor to the representative of Israel. Mr. Fedorenko, in a point of order, felt that it was not appropriate to call on him because "he has lied enough before this Council, and that it will not be a great loss if he will generally refrain from any further statements here and from a continuation of lies which have been proved to be lies." The President explained that he had to call on the speakers in the order in which they were inscribed on his list. Mr. Fedorenko made a second point of order:

> "As is the custom on such occasions, I would say in all modesty that I would expect from you as President more understanding and more desire to take into account the severe reality which has been created by those on whom you again wish to call."

Two more points of order were made by Mr. Goldberg and Mr. Fedorenko until, finally, the representative of Israel could begin his speech. After his second sentence, he was interrupted by a point of order made by the representative of Bulgaria who felt that the representative of Israel "diverts the attention" of the Security Council from the subject. Mr. Tarabanov stated that "if the representative of Israel is going to talk to the Council, he must speak as in the prisoner's dock on the aggression that was committed." The representative of Israel, Mr. Gideon Rafael, said—after having been interrupted by this point of order and a statement of the President "that we would all be interested in continuing our discussion in dignity and that we all should concentrate, as far as possible, on the issues which we are discussing"—

> "I am not here as the accused party; I am not here in the dock, and the representative of Bulgaria has not been appointed as a prosecutor."

Very soon, Mr. Tarabanov again asked the President to call Mr. Rafael to order. He finally was permitted to speak without further interruption, as were the representatives of Jordan and Syria.

At 2:30 in the morning, Ambassador Goldberg took the floor:

> "It is 2:30 in the morning and I do not intend to take the time of the Council to review all that has happened in the last several days. I have a very brief comment to make. My friend, Ambassador Fedorenko, complains that I have been silent. He speaks so frequently and at such length that it is quite difficult to get a word in."

The Secretary-General reported on the situation. Mr. Tarabanov had again attacked "the arrogance of the brigand when he knows that the judge in the court that is to try him is bought." He said that the criminal has "found accomplices among the judges." He added: "And what a judge."

At 2:39, when the Secretary-General finished his report, the meeting was adjourned. It was almost Sunday morning. Only a few hours later, Ambassador Tabor, the President of the Council for the month of June, had to call another emergency meeting.

* * *

The Security Council was convened on Sunday, June 11,

THE WAR IN THE MIDDLE EAST 1967

at 10:30 p.m. The representative of the Syrian Arab Republic, Mr. Tomeh, spoke first:

> "Mr. President, I wish to thank you and the members of the Council for having responded to our appeal to hold this urgent emergency meeting of the Security Council. I must say that in view of the fact that today is Sunday, which is a day of rest, the inconvenience that this meeting is causing to the members of the Council and to you is undoubtedly great. But perhaps an excuse can be found in the fact that the situation we are facing is getting graver and graver every day, and is deteriorating to an extent which I am sure will not be accepted by the Security Council."

He then complained that Israeli forces were not respecting the cease-fire, had occupied the town of Rafid, and were aiming at the Yarmuk River. The representative of Israel, Mr. Rafael, immediately denied these claims, stating that there was no fighting whatsoever anywhere along the front line.

Mr. Fedorenko felt that the Israeli denial was meaningless. "The ruling circles of Israel," he said, "are making a mockery of the United Nations Organization, and of the Security Council and its decisions." In his opinion, a report submitted by the Secretary-General confirmed movements of Israeli tank columns in the area, and this caused him to attack Israel vehemently:

> "From the statement of the Secretary-General just made, it is clear that United Nations Observers have witnessed movements of tank columns in the area, but as was to be expected, from Tel Aviv once again we received an immediate denial of this new violation by the Israeli occupation forces of the decisions of the Security Council. From this it is clear that the Tel

Aviv adventurists are deliberately continuing to misinform and delude this august body.

We ask, is this cynical defiance to be tolerated, this outrageous lying? How long is this flagrant trickery to go on, this flouting of the Security Council's decisions? How long are certain representatives here, the patrons of the international adventurists in Tel Aviv, going to continue their sabotage, their paralyzing of the work of this Council, which is unable to take its proper decisions?"

Lord Caradon of the United Kingdom observed that the representative of Israel "has told us that there has been no advance beyond the cease-fire line." He suggested "that what we can do, what we should do, and what we must do is to make absolutely clear, tonight, now, that we insist that there should be no breach whatsoever of the cease-fire."

Mr. Keita of the Mali delegation then turned on the Security Council:

> "Day follows day and night follows night, and the Council continues to meet to discuss the grave situation prevailing at present in the Middle East. However, despite this proliferation of meetings—meetings which the entire world is following very closely—it appears that the Security Council is unable to arrive at a decision.
>
> My delegation believes that the Council is showing an impotence that is not worthy of it. It would appear that some occult force is slowing down and is stopping in the Council any possibility or movement towards decision. With regret, I note and I must state that this attitude on the part of the Council at these grave hours, and in the light of the situation which is only worsening in the Middle East, is, to put it mildly, not only shameful, but unworthy of our Organization. For too much time we have shown the painful spectacle not

THE WAR IN THE MIDDLE EAST 1967

only of an impotent body, but of a body that is showing passive complicity with everything that saps the prestige of the United Nations."

Other speakers continued to attack each other and the Council, which caused the following observation by Ambassador Goldberg:

> "I am becoming more and more convinced that if we are to have an effective cease-fire on the ground—a cease-fire which both Syria and Israel have agreed to—we will first have to agree upon a cease-fire of words in this Council."

The "cease-fire of words" did not materialize, but at 3 a.m. the Security Council unanimously adopted a draft resolution which condemned "any and all violations of the cease-fire," affirmed "that its demand for a cease-fire and discontinuance of all military activities includes a prohibition of any forward military movements subsequent to the cease-fire," and called "for the prompt return to the cease-fire positions of any troops which may have moved forward subsequent to 1630 hours GMT, 10 June." Another meeting of the Security Council was supposed to be held at 5 p.m. on the same day. It was already Monday morning when the President declared that on the basis of his consultations "the final decision on the timing will be taken later today."

The meeting did not take place until Tuesday, June 13, 1967, at 3 p.m. The meeting lasted six hours; it was called on a written request of the Soviet delegation and did not produce any results. Ambassador Fedorenko fought for the adoption of the following draft resolution:

> *"The Security Council,*
> *Noting* that Israel, in defiance of the Security Council's resolution on the cessation of military activities and a cease-

fire has seized additional territory of the United Arab Republic, Jordan and Syria,

Noting that although military activities have now ceased, Israel is still occupying the territory of those countries, thus failing to halt its aggression and defying the United Nations and all peace-loving States,

Considering unacceptable and unlawful Israel's territorial claims on Arab States,

1. *Vigorously condemns* Israel's aggressive activities and continued occupation of part of the territory of the United Arab Republic, Syria and Jordan, regarding this as an act of aggression and the grossest violation of the United Nations Charter and generally recognized principles of international law;

2. *Demands* that Israel should immediately and unconditionally remove all its troops from the territory of those States and withdraw them behind the armistice lines and should respect the status of the demilitarized zones, as prescribed in the General Armistice Agreements."

Ambassador Goldberg felt that this resolution "cannot lead toward peace. It is rather a big step backward towards another war." He advocated the adoption of another resolution which would "call for discussions among the parties concerned, using such third party or United Nations assistance as they may wish, looking toward the establishment of viable arrangements encompassing the withdrawal and disengagement of armed personnel, the renunciation of force regardless of its nature, the maintenance of vital international rights and the establishment of a stable and durable peace in the Middle East. (S/7952/Rev. 2)."

In an atmosphere of mounting tension the meeting recessed at 9:20 p.m. and a new meeting was called to order at 10:00 p.m. This meeting heard addresses by the representa-

THE WAR IN THE MIDDLE EAST 1967

tives of Syria and Jordan. Mr. Goldberg exercised his right of reply, and the Council recessed until the next day. On June 14, 1967, the vote was finally taken. Only the Soviet draft resolution was put to a vote because the United States draft resolution was not "pressed to a vote."

The vote was first on Operative Paragraph 1 of the Soviet proposal. In favor: Bulgaria, India, Mali and the Soviet Union. Against: none. Abstentions were recorded by Argentina, Brazil, Canada, China, Denmark, Ethiopia, France, Japan, Nigeria, the United Kingdom and the United States. The President announced that Operative Paragraph 1 had not been adopted.

After the vote, the President apologized to the Soviet Union because, contrary to the rules of procedure, he had forgotten to ask the Soviet representative before the vote whether he agreed to a separate vote on the individual paragraphs of his draft resolution. Mr. Fedorenko accepted this procedure. Mr. Goldberg then observed that "in the most trying of circumstances the President of the Council has conducted himself with complete fidelity to the rules of procedure and has attempted to the best of his ability, which has been extraordinary, to preside impartially and to carry out the wishes of the Council."

This praise prompted the Soviet representative to take the floor again:

> "Allow me to say that I did not quite understand the words just spoken by the United States representative. What is this sworn statement? Why do we need this lawyer's brief? We are engaged in a dialogue, Mr. President, a normal dialogue full of tact. We understand each other, but why do others act as they do? I have the impression that someone becomes deaf at

a given point, deaf from the political standpoint, of course. But the deaf answer very fast, but sometimes not very much to the point."

The United States representative responded: "I do not think that the Soviet representative has to tell me what to say; I do not tell him what to say." The President declared "that this dialogue has now finished" and put the second operative paragraph of the Soviet draft resolution to a vote. This paragraph received two more votes. In addition to the previous supporters, Ethiopia and Nigeria voted for it. Six votes, however, did not suffice, and Operative Paragraph 2 was not adopted, nor was the draft resolution adopted as a whole.

Needless to say, the irritation of the members of the Council did not subside after the vote. The meeting was adjourned at 3:25 p.m. At 5:50 a new meeting was called to order at which a draft resolution sponsored by Argentina, Brazil and Ethiopia, recommending to the Governments concerned that they scrupulously respect the humanitarian principles governing the treatment of prisoners of war, was unanimously adopted. When the representative of Israel, Mr. Kidron, wanted to take the floor after the vote was taken, the Soviet representative made the following point of order:

"I take the floor to remind you, Mr. President, that too many speeches have been uttered in the Council by the representatives of Israel, and we have said what value there was in these statements. The representative of Israel has tried to delude, to deceive, the Council. He was unmasked. This was confirmed by objective proof contained in the report of the Secretary-General, U Thant."

THE WAR IN THE MIDDLE EAST 1967

Mr. Fedorenko did not succeed in preventing Mr. Kidron from speaking. His remarks showed, however, that the tension in the Security Council was rapidly approaching a point of complete paralysis.

* * *

A day before, on June 13, 1967, the Soviet Ambassador had written the following letter to Secretary-General U Thant:

Letter dated 13 June 1967 from the Permanent Representative of the Union of Soviet Socialist Republics to the United Nations adressed to the Secretary-General. (A/6717).

His Excellency U Thant
Secretary-General of the United Nations
I have the honour to forward herewith a letter from Mr. A.A. Gromyko, Minister for Foreign Affairs of the USSR, concerning the immediate convening of an emergency special session of the General Assembly to consider the question of liquidating the consequences of Israel's aggression against the Arab States and the immediate withdrawal of Israel's troops behind the armistice lines.

(*Signed*) N. Fedorenko

* * *

Letter from Andrei Gromyko, Minister for Foreign Affairs of the Union of Soviet Socialist Republics, to the Secretary-General of the United Nations.
Despite the Security Council's decisions concerning the cessation of hostilities between Israel and the Arab States, Israel is continuing its piratical aggression. In flagrant defiance of the Security Council demands for a cease-fire adopted on 6,

WAR ON WAR

7 and 9 June, Israel has seized further territories belonging to the United Arab Republic, Jordan and Syria.

The Soviet Government considers it essential that the United Nations General Assembly, in accordance with Article 11 of the United Nations Charter, should consider the situation which has arisen and should adopt a decision designed to bring about the liquidation of the consequences of aggression and the immediate withdrawal of Israel forces behind the armistice lines.

The Soviet Government calls for the immediate convening of an emergency special session of the United Nations General Assembly for these purposes. The Soviet Government proposes that an emergency special session should be convened within twenty-four hours.

The Soviet Government requests you to take whatever steps are necessary for the convening of such a session and to notify it as promptly as possible of the exact date of opening of the General Assembly's session. The Soviet Government would inform you that it will send a delegation including leading statesmen of the Soviet Union to the General Assembly.

Kindly regard this letter as an explanatory memorandum within the meaning of Rule 20 of the Rules of Procedure and circulate it without delay as an official document of the United Nations General Assembly.

(*Signed*) A. Gromyko
Minister for Foreign Affairs of the USSR

* * *

The Special Emergency Session of the General Assembly began its deliberations on June 17. No further action on the part of the Security Council was therefore possible.

On September 18, the (Fifth) Emergency Special Session came to an end. No practical results were obtained.

THE WAR IN THE MIDDLE EAST 1967

The President, Ambassador Pazhwak of Afghanistan, expressed it clearly in his concluding statement:

> "Before we bring these proceedings to an end I believe that it would be appropriate for me, as Presiding Officer, to record very briefly two impressions resulting from our deliberations.
> In the first place, I consider that there has been remarkably strong emphasis given to the great importance of the problem which it has been our task to consider, and to the urgency of finding a proper and just solution.
> Secondly, the Assembly has agreed that the solution to the grave situation in the Middle East which occasioned this emergency special session must belong in the United Nations."

Could even the greatest optimist find in these words any hint of a true achievement by the General Assembly?

CHAPTER FIVE

THE PUEBLO INCIDENT

ON JANUARY 25, 1968, the permanent representative of the United States of America addressed the following letter to the President of the Security Council:

"I request an urgent meeting of the Security Council to consider the grave threat to peace which has been brought about by a series of increasingly dangerous and aggressive military actions by North Korean authorities in violation of the Armistice Agreement, of international law and of the Charter of the United Nations.

The armistice regime established by the Armistice Agreement of 27 July 1953 has been repeatedly violated by North Korean authorities. These violations have become increasingly serious during the past year and a half, during which armed personnel on many occasions have been dispatched from North Korea across the demilitarized zone into the Republic of Korea on missions of terrorism and political assassination. A particularly grave incident occurred this month, when a band of armed terrorists was dispatched into the Republic of Korea on a mission whose apparent goal was the assassination of President Park.

More recently, North Korea has wilfully committed an act of wanton lawlessness against a naval vessel of the United States operating on the high seas. On 23 January, the *USS*

THE PUEBLO INCIDENT

Pueblo, while operating in international waters, was illegally seized by armed North Korean vessels, and the ship and crew are still under forcible detention by North Korean authorities.

This North Korean action against a United States naval vessel on the high seas, and the serious North Korean armed raids across the demilitarized zone into the Republic of Korea, have created a situation of such gravity and danger as to require the urgent consideration of the Security Council which we are accordingly requesting.

Please accept, etc.

(*Signed*) Arthur J. Goldberg"

Agha Shahi of Pakistan, the President of the Security Council for the month of January, convened the Council at 3:30 p.m. on January 26, 1968.

When the meeting was opened, the representative of the Soviet Union, Platon Morozov, opposed the adoption of the agenda. He felt that "any request for a meeting of the Council is nothing but a manoeuvre of the United States in a most unworthy enterprise." He called the accusations of the United States against the Democratic People's Republic of Korea "slanderous" and said that the attempt to draw the Security Council into a consideration of these accusations would "aggravate the tension in the Korean peninsula" and "threaten further the cause of peace and security in that part of the world."

U.S. representative Arthur J. Goldberg, in his reply, alluded to Alice in Wonderland. He said that the Soviet Union passed judgment before hearing the evidence: "In Alice in Wonderland terms: 'Sentence first, trial afterwards.'" But, he said, "what may be characteristic of Soviet justice is not practice and tradition of this Council."

WAR ON WAR

Ambassador Goldberg's optimism and trust in the Security Council was expressed in his words:

> "We have sought an urgent meeting of the Council because of our belief and conviction that if it is at all possible this situation should be dealt with and settled peacefully through diplomatic channels. Clearly, the primary diplomatic channel in the world today is the Security Council, the organ of this Organization with primary responsibility for the maintenance of international peace and security.
>
> We shall be quite content to have the Council judge the merits of the situation after hearing about the situation. But whatever anyone's views are, or may be, about the merits of this situation, it would be completely incomprehensible, and I believe intolerable, to men of peace throughout the world if this Council were to shun its duty and to refuse to deal with this grave situation."

His opinion was shared by the representatives of Canada and the United Kingdom. Ambassador Ignatieff of Canada said that his delegation "is conscious of the heavy responsibility which the Security Council was meant to exercise and should exercise when problems arise relating to the maintenance of international peace and security." The primary issue in this case was "whether the Council will take advantage of this opportunity to discharge its primary responsibility for the maintenance of international peace and security." And he observed that "the fact that one of the major Powers in the world should today be seeking the assistance of the United Nations in overcoming a difficult problem through diplomatic channels is surely something that should be welcomed by the Security Council . . ."

THE PUEBLO INCIDENT

Sir Leslie Glass of the United Kingdom formulated the problem in even clearer terms:

> "Article 1, Chapter I of the United Nations Charter sets out the first purpose of our Organization as being to maintain international peace and security. Article 24 of the Charter, sub-paragraph 1, sets out that the Members of the United Nations confer on the Security Council primary responsibility for the maintenance of international peace and security.
>
> In this dangerous age, in many ways more dangerous than when the Charter was written, the members of the Security Council have an immense responsibility in the fearful issues of war and peace.
>
> We have now before us a grave situation. No one who has studied the facts can fail to feel blowing here the chill wind of authentic danger. The world man-in-the-street does not have to be a brilliant diplomatist or military expert to see the obvious risks involved if this matter cannot be settled peacefully. Certainly it can be settled peacefully, but to achieve this the Security Council must play its proper part. It will surely be inconceivable to the peoples of the world if the Security Council of the United Nations does not urgently consider the question now put before it."

Sir Leslie recalled the sad experience of the second Middle East war:

> "Many of us here worked in the Security Council through the long hot summer of the Arab-Israel war, whose dangerous consequences still remain an anxious burden on the world. When the situation which led to this war was building up there was some talk of 'over-dramatization' of the situation,

and a reluctance to get down to what is our clearly defined primary job of tackling issues of international security. The resulting delay had, my delegation believes, most serious consequences. We shall not easily be forgiven by world opinion if we make the same mistake again."

This did not convince the representatives of Hungary and the Soviet Union. Mr. Csatorday of Hungary felt that "by bringing this whole matter before the Security Council, the United States is reverting to a very old practice of sharing the responsibility—which it should bear itself for its actions—with the Security Council, with the United Nations, thus usurping the name of our Organization and of our Council." He did not explain how such usurpation was being performed by presenting a problem to the Security Council. Obviously, the letter sent by the U.S. representative to the President of the Security Council was, in his opinion, not a proper presentation. "It creates further misunderstanding and further trouble and, besides, casts a very heavy shadow over the work of our Organization and does not promote peaceful co-operation or strengthen the cause of international peace." The Hungarian representative did not elaborate on how the U.S. letter could "cast a very heavy shadow" over the work of the United Nations, since it was only a suggestion to place a certain problem on the agenda of the Security Council. Such a suggestion only expressed the opinion of the United States; further action belonged to the Council.

Ambassador Morozov, in his second series of remarks, also opposed the presentation of the problem in the American letter of January 25: "If there were any doubt concerning the true intentions behind this letter, the representative of the

THE PUEBLO INCIDENT

United States was rather helpful to those who still nurture any doubts or illusions."

We discussed here in detail the various arguments advanced in the procedural discussion in the Security Council on the adoption of the agenda because this discussion, more than the ensuing battle on the substance of the matter, revealed the opinions of the role of the Security Council in general. The American, Canadian and British representatives felt that, according to the United Nations Charter, the dispute with the Democratic People's Republic of Korea (North Korea) ought to be settled by the Security Council. The Soviet and Hungarian representatives felt that, due to an improper presentation of the suggested item on the agenda, the Security Council should simply ignore the request of one party to the conflict.

The agenda was adopted by twelve votes to three (Soviet Union, Algeria and Hungary).

Ambassador Goldberg presented the case. With the aid of maps, he showed that the *USS Pueblo* had been seized by the North Korean vessels in international waters. He then referred to the infiltrations from North Korea and the terrorist campaign of its government, which had "reached a new level of outrage." He made no concrete proposal, however, concerning action by the Security Council. He said only that he asked "with all earnestness the Security Council to rectify this dangerous situation and eliminate this threat to peace." How this could be done, the U.S. representative did not say. He concluded:

> "This great and potent Organization of peace must not let the cause of peace in Korea be lost by default to the highhanded tactics of a lawless regime. Such a course would be

an invitation to catastrophe. Therefore, let the Security Council, with its great influence, promptly and effectively help to secure forthwith the safe return of the *Pueblo* and its crew; and to restore to full vigour and effectiveness the Korean Armistice Agreement."

Ambassador Morozov of the Soviet Union immediately challenged the facts and the approach of his American colleague. Concerning the maps, he said, he "actually did not want to tax his visual abilities." He was "not very interested in the whole trip of the *Pueblo* and the various points where it may have been at one time or another." The ship was in the territorial waters of the Democratic People's Republic of Korea. The point mentioned in a co-ordinate for the location of the ship "was not mentioned in the remarkable professorial lecture" of the U.S. representative.

An exchange of arguments ensued in the exercise of the right of reply. Both representatives, as lawyers by profession, used their legal skills. Goldberg remainded Morozov that he ought to be "well familiar with the old rule of law that it is the contemporary account at the time which is entitled to weight, not a subsequent one which may be invented to suit the needs of the party involved." The co-ordinate for the location of the ship was released by the North Korean authorities quite some time after the ship had been seized.

The discussion continued during the next meeting, on January 27. Lord Caradon of the United Kingdom, Lij Endalkachew Makonnen of Ethiopia, Csatorday of Hungary and Ignatieff of Canada presented their views, whereupon Goldberg and Morozov again exercised their right of reply.

Lord Caradon mentioned in his speech that "often when we meet in this Council to consider a dispute or a conflict we

THE PUEBLO INCIDENT

have to endeavour to work out a framework for a settlement. Sometimes we have succeeded in doing so, as we did recently in regard to the Middle East." He did not care to say what was the framework for a settlement in the Middle East. As far as Korea was concerned, he referred to the Armistice Agreement which had been reached fifteen years before and accepted by all parties. The Ethiopian representative expressed confidence in the Security Council. "Experience has clearly shown," he said, "that when the Council has been given a fair chance and a breathing spell to exert its healing influence through the proper use of good offices, and when all sides to a dispute have been willing to co-operate, the Council can have the capacity and the means to play its vital role of averting imminent danger to international peace."

The Hungarian representative repeatedly quoted *The New York Times*, as did Mr. Morozov in his reply to Mr. Goldberg. The U.S. Ambassador then again asked for the floor to exercise his right of reply:

> "I am very glad that our colleague, Ambassador Morozov, is such an assiduous reader of *The New York Times* and I am glad that he shares my high regard for that eminent and world-famous newspaper. But if you are as assiduous a reader of *The New York Times* as I am, you start on page 1 and not on the much later page to which Ambassador Morozov referred. And since he, as I said yesterday, is such a distinguished lawyer, he will remember another legal rule: that you must not merely excerpt quotations, you must give the whole record and not a partial one."

Mr. Goldberg then quoted from *The New York Times* of the very same day (January 27, 1968), an article on page 1 according to which a Soviet vessel, the *Gidrolog,* was shadowing the American aircraft carrier *Enterprise* off the South Korean coast. The *Gidrolog* was on the same sort of mission as the one in which the *Pueblo* had been engaged. The quotation, said Mr. Goldberg, "illustrates that by picking selected excerpts you can come to one conclusion, but when you read the whole article, then, as it appears, you arrive at another conclusion." Mr. Morozov, in his previous reply, had quoted another article, on page 7 of *The New York Times* from the same day, according to which Secretary of State Rusk had stated to the Senate Foreign Relations Committee that "he could not be categorical" about the position of the *Pueblo* at the time when it was seized. Ambassador Goldberg corrected the misinterpretation of this quotation on page 7 by quoting sentences omitted by Ambassador Morozov.

The Soviet representative immediately replied:

". . . I shall confine myself to a brief reply to the new lengthy quotations and excursions which the representative of the United States has made once again for a fourth, perhaps fifth time—I do not know how many—in an attempt to lend an appearance of some cogency or at least plausibility to that one-sided and unfounded version which he is continuing so insistently to put forward; I am ready to read, of course, the first, second and third pages of *The New York Times*. I did so immediately the newspaper appeared—the ink was still wet, in fact, on its pages."

He assured that he "did not wrench anything out of context" and had "distorted nothing." And he resorted to his lawyer's arsenal:

THE PUEBLO INCIDENT

"Justice Goldberg knows very well that after a witness has given evidence in a high court, then the worst moment of all comes for that witness. The procedure which is followed in criminal legislation in all countries throughout the world is called cross-examination. The purpose of cross-examination is not only to hear what the witness says but to give the parties and the judge the right to ask clarifying questions. With his great legal experience the representative of the United States cannot fail to know that very often, after brilliant testimony on the part of witnesses which it would appear leaves no doubt whatsoever as to what really happened, the decisive point and one which sometimes annihilates the whole value of that testimony is the answer to the questions which are given for purposes of clarification in the course of the procedure that I mentioned."

Morozov explained, after this introduction, that he had previously permitted himself "to refer to that part which has a direct bearing on the reply to that clarifying question." He did not hear it said here "that such question had not been put in the course of the procedure" which he had just mentioned. "If that question was put," he continued in his obviously complicated argumentation, "then some answer was given other than the one to which the fresh pages of today's issue of *The New York Times* bear witness." And he added: "I emphasize—concerning the present clarifying question."

Goldberg probably needed more time to understand the direct bearing of the "clarifying question" on the reply, for this time he remained silent.

The President then said that the Council had heard "full statements from the representatives of the United States and the Soviet Union setting forth their respective versions of the situation confronting the Security Council." There was no exaggeration in Mr. Shahi's resumé. He added that "the time

WAR ON WAR

has now come for the Council to consider how it should proceed to meet the situation facing it."

Finally he said: "The representative of Canada has proposed that the members of the Council utilize the weekend to enter into consultations. Therefore, as there is no objection, I now propose to adjourn the Council until Monday afternoon in order to permit consultations among the members." The meeting adjourned at 1:35 p.m.

* * *

Monday, January 29, no meeting of the Security Council was convened. Another two weeks passed before the Council met. On February 16, 1968, a new President, Ambassador Solano Lopez of Paraguay, opened the next meeting of the Security Council with the usual tribute to his predecessor who, he said, had been called upon "to preside over the Council in trying circumstances, which made it necessary for him to display his outstanding qualities, his talent, his patience, his wisdom and his diplomacy."

The problem of North Korea and the *USS Pueblo* was no longer on the agenda of this meeting. The annals of the United Nations are silent about the consultations which were supposed to have begun on the weekend of January 27. It is left for the future historian to guess whether they ever began. *The New York Times* did not report on it, neither on page 1 nor on page 7 of its subsequent issues. Fortunately, a second Korean War has not broken out by the time of this writing. Claiming that this fact is due to the efforts of the Security Council or that the danger of such war has disappeared would be to display an excess of optimism, to which, based on historical experience, no one is really entitled.

CHAPTER SIX

THE CZECHOSLOVAKIAN CRISIS

EARLY IN THE MORNING of August 21, 1968, Radio Prague made the following announcement:

"Last night, August 20, about 11 p.m., the armies of the Soviet Union, the Polish People's Republic, the German Democratic Republic, the Hungarian People's Republic and the Bulgarian People's Republic crossed the national frontiers of Czechoslovakia without the knowledge of the President of the Republic, the National Assembly, the Government, the First Secretary of the Communist Party or any of their bodies.

Almost simultaneously with this broadcast—after which Radio Prague went off the air—troop-carrying transport planes arrived at Ruzyne International Airport. Within seven hours a full airborne division had landed in Prague. Two hours earlier a column of tanks had crossed the frontier from East Germany into Czechoslovakia.
When the news reached the capitals of the world, the Governments of the United States, the United Kingdom, France, Canada, Denmark and Paraguay, all members of the

WAR ON WAR

Security Council, requested, through their representatives at the United Nations, an emergency meeting of the Council. The President for the month of August, Ambassador de Araujo Castro, of Brazil, called the meeting for 5:30 p.m. that same day.

After calling the meeting to order, the President of the Council gave the floor to the Soviet Ambassador, Yakov Malik, who read a letter addressed to the President by the Soviet delegation:

"Mr. President,
The Government of the United States of America and some other countries—their allies—sent you a letter which contains a request to convene a meeting of the Security Council to consider the question of the present situation in the Czechoslovak Socialist Republic.

Yet there is no basis for the discussion of this matter by the Security Council. The armed units of the socialist countries, as is well known, entered the territory of the Czechoslovak Socialist Republic on the basis of the request of the Government of that State, which applied to the allied Governments for assistance, including assistance with armed forces, in view of the threats created by the external and internal reaction to the socialist system and to the statehood established by the Constitution of Czechoslovakia. The Soviet Government and the Governments of other allied States have decided to meet the request of the Czechoslovak Government for military assistance in accordance with the existing treaty obligations and on the basis of the relevant provisions of the United Nations Charter.

It goes without saying that the above-mentioned armed units will be immediately withdrawn from the territory of the Czechoslovak Socialist Republic as soon as the existing threat

THE CZECHOSLOVAKIAN CRISIS

to the security is eliminated and the lawful authorities find that the further presence there of those armed units is no longer necessary.

The actions of the Soviet Union and other socialist countries are dictated by the care for the strengthening of peace and the non-admissibility of undermining the mainstays of European security. Attempts to present these actions in a different light can by no means change our peaceful intentions or diminish the rights of the socialist countries to individual and collective self-defence.

The Soviet Government has repeatedly warned that the attempts of imperialist reaction to interfere in the domestic affairs of the Czechoslovak Socialist Republic and in relations among the socialist countries will not be tolerated and will meet with a resolute rebuff.

The Soviet Government takes this opportunity again to call upon all States strictly to observe the principles of respect for sovereignty and independence and of the inadmissibility of aggression, direct or indirect, against other States and peoples.

Upon the instructions of the Soviet Government, I inform you, Mr. President, that the Soviet Union resolutely opposes the consideration of this question in the Security Council because this would be in the interests of certain external circles, the forces of aggression. The events in Czechoslovakia are a matter of concern for the Czechoslovak people and the States of the socialist community, linked among themselves by appropriate mutual obligations."

This letter prompted a discussion on the adoption of the agenda. The American representative, Ambassador George Ball, reminded the Council that the request (to place the situation in Czechoslovakia upon the agenda) was "proper

WAR ON WAR

. . . and its inscription should be promptly effected if the Council is to live up to the responsibilities given it by the Charter." He then proceeded to go into the merits of the request:

> "The situation the world faces tonight is an affront to all civilized sensibilities. Foreign armies have without warning invaded a Member State of the United Nations. If the Security Council does not seize itself of this gross violation of the Charter and deal with it promptly and incisively, its vitality and integrity, its very seriousness of purpose, will be subject to serious question.
>
> Rarely has a situation come before the Council where the ugly facts of aggression have been written so large and in such unmistakable characters. The Soviet Union has arrogantly announced to the world that it has sent its armies into Czechoslovakia, and the evidence is beyond question that it and its client States have done so in order to impose by force a repressive political system which is plainly obnoxious to the people and leadership of Czechoslovakia.
>
> The Soviet Union and its Eastern European accomplices have not even tried to conceal the fact of this invasion. How could they? Rather—in a feeble and futile effort at self-justification—they have fabricated the claim that this invasion was requested by Czechoslovakia, with the contention that what we confront is an internal matter which is none of the business of the Security Council. We all know that this claim is a fraud, an inept and obvious fraud."

When Ambassador Ball, continuing to discuss the situation in Czechoslovakia, quoted a late communiqué issued by the various Communist parties in Bratislava, he was interrupted on points of order by the representatives of Hungary and, later, of the Soviet Union, who demanded a strictly

THE CZECHOSLOVAKIAN CRISIS

procedural debate. The President of the Council disagreed. Taking the floor again, Ball said that "it is perfectly normal when Governments sponsor the inscribing of an item on the agenda that they explain the reasons why they do." And he went on:

> "I can well understand, I may say, why the representative of the Soviet Union is disturbed by my quoting the Bratislava communiqué—I should be ashamed of it if I were he under those circumstances also."

Ball quoted Radio Prague which clearly stated that the invasion had taken place without the knowledge of the President and the other official leaders of the Czechoslovak Republic. He also mentioned that the Czechoslovak Mission to the United Nations had released a declaration by the Czechoslovak Ministry of Foreign Affairs protesting against the action of the Soviet Union "with the requirement that the illegal occupation of Czechoslovakia be stopped without delay and all armed troops be withdrawn from Czechoslovakia." An additional declaration, he said further, had been issued by the deputies of the National Assembly protesting against the occupation of Czechoslovakia and calling on all people not to resort to forcible action against the occupation armies. The declaration ended with the appeal:

> "Working people, citizens! Remain on your working places and protect your enterprises. For further development of socialism in Czechoslovakia make use of all democratic means. If necessary, you will be able to defend yourself also by a general strike. We are confident that we will overcome these serious moments with pride and character."

WAR ON WAR

Ambassador Ball discussed at considerable length the claim that the armed units of the Soviet Union and the other socialist countries had entered the territory of Czechoslovakia "on the basis of the request of the Government of that State." He said that an effort was being made "to create the patently false impression that the Czechoslovak Government was requesting its own destruction and the Czechoslovak peoples were asking for the occupation of their country." It was clear, Ball continued, that "the duly constituted leaders of the Czechoslovak Government, the President of the Republic, the Chairman of the National Assembly, the Premier and even the First Secretary of the Czechoslovak Communist Party Central Committee made no such request." If the Soviet leaders had heard voices calling on them to invade Czechoslovakia, Ball said, they were "the voices of a new breed of quislings." He felt that the Council would "not take much time to dispose of this doomed and desperate effort to frustrate its procedures." He urged the immediate adoption of the agenda challenged by the Soviet Union, in order "to condemn this brazen violation of the United Nations Charter and to call on the Soviet Union and its allies to withdraw its forces immediately from Czechoslovakia."

Ambassador Ball was supported by his colleagues from Canada, the United Kingdom and Denmark, all of whom agreed that the Security Council had to take action. Lord Caradon of the United Kingdom even expressed "a sense of compassion" for Ambassador Malik for having "to defend such a disgraceful act."

The Soviet Ambassador, however, declined to accept such courtesies. He stated again that the armed forces of the Socialist States "had entered the territory of Czechoslovakia as a result of a request of the Government of that State." He turned on Mr. Ball, accusing him of attempts to voice slanderous insinuations. In reply to Lord Caradon's expression of sympathy, he said that he, Malik, had "many more reasons not to envy you in the role you are playing today," because his speech had been "disgusting" and "hypocritical." Ambassador Malik sharply attacked the United States and the other powers which had raised the matter in the Security Council. "The reason for this imperialist action," he said, "is to continue to foster the efforts of the counter-revolutionary struggle and the hostile campaign against socialist Czechoslovakia, against its working class, against its people."

When the President proposed a vote on the adoption of the agenda, a strange situation developed. Ambassador Malik opposed taking a vote, maintaining that although he had "stated that there were no grounds for discussion of this matter in the Security Council," he had concluded that the Soviet delegation did "not insist on a vote in this matter." Ambassador Ball felt, however, that "it would be only appropriate, in spite of the last statement of the representative of the Soviet Union, that the Council be asked to express its view on this matter."

The President again announced that "since objections have been raised to the adoption of the agenda," he intended to proceed to a vote. Ambassador Malik again intervened:

> "When the one who objects does not insist on a vote things may not be pushed as far as a vote. The one who objected set out his position in his statement and this suffices."

However, Ambassador Ball requested a vote. Finally, after one more interruption by the Soviet Ambassador, the vote was taken. Thirteen members of the Security Council voted in favor of the adoption; two (Hungary and the Soviet Union) were opposed.

The agenda was adopted. The representatives of Algeria, India and Pakistan explained that their votes favoring adoption of the agenda had no bearing upon the merits of the question. Ambassador de Araujo Castro, the President, then made a surprise announcement. He informed the Security Council that he had received a letter from the Permanent Representative of Czechoslovakia requesting an invitation to participate in the deliberations of the Security Council. In accordance with customary practice, the request was granted, and Jan Muzik, alternate representative of Czechoslovakia, took a seat at the table. He was immediately given the floor and he read several messages which had been received in the course of the day from the Czech Minister of Foreign Affairs. The messages gave an account of the day's events and a protest by the Minister of Foreign Affairs against "the illegal occupation of Czechoslovakia." Ten Ministers had signed a statement that they considered the occupation of Czechoslovakia, "which took place without accord or knowledge of the Czechoslovak Government, as illegal, contrary to international law and Socialist internationalism." The Presidium of the Czechoslovak National Assembly had issued a declaration containing six points, the fourth of which was an appeal to the Parliaments of all countries and to world public opinion "to support our legitimate requirements." Finally, the President of the Republic, Ludvik Svoboda, had made an appeal on the radio, stating that Soviet, Polish, Bulgarian, East German and Hungarian military units had entered Czechoslovakia "without the consent of the constitutional organs of the State." These organs, the President of the Czechoslovak Republic said over the radio,

THE CZECHOSLOVAKIAN CRISIS

"must expeditiously solve the situation that has arisen and attain an early withdrawal of foreign troops."

After Muzik had brought these messages to the attention of the Security Council, the debate began. The representatives of the United States, Canada, France and Denmark called for a withdrawal of all foreign troops from Czechoslovakia. On Yakov Malik fell the burden of defending the step taken by the Soviet Union and its allies. He declared at the outset:

> "It goes without saying that we shall call a spade a spade, especially taking into account the torrent of slander and insinuations with which the new United States representative in the Security Council has spoken today."

He read to the Council an appeal of "the lawful legitimate authorities in the country" addressed to the "allied States, including the Soviet Union, with an insistent demand for direct immediate assistance to the Czechoslovak people, including assistance through armed forces." Ambassador Malik said that the appeal had come from "a group of members of the Central Committee, of the Government and the National Assembly," but mentioned no names. This appeal takes up over seven pages in the Verbatim Record of the 1441st meeting of the Security Council. "This is the appeal," said Malik, "which caused us to heed it and to come to the assistance of Czechoslovakia and its armed forces." He then began to quote statements by various American politicians expressing sympathy with certain trends that had manifested themselves in Czechoslovakia prior to the occupation by Soviet troops. He read excerpts from articles in the *Wall Street Journal* and *Frankfurter Allgemeine Zeitung* asserting that they advocated interference by Western Powers in the affairs of Czechoslovakia. In sharp language he attacked Ambassador Ball:

> "As a matter of fact, the statement of Ambassador Ball is a clear-cut example of open and direct incitement to those forces (*i.e.* "to the reactionaries and the forces of the counter-revolution") to exert new efforts to bring down the social system in Czechoslovakia, incitement to an open struggle for power on the part of those forces. It is a signal for bloodletting, for internecine, fratricidal struggle in the Czechoslovak Socialist Republic."

When Malik had concluded his lengthy statement, his American colleague, exercising his right of reply, said:

> "One of my instructions is to try to understand the position of the Soviet Union. I have therefore listened with great patience and attention to the statements of the Soviet representative. They are very impressive statements from a quantitative point of view. The are very impressive also in the astonishingly wide range of irrelevance which they contain . . .
>
> The Soviet representative . . . has read a very long and somewhat incoherent statement from a nameless group, but I do not know who they are and he has not told us. They are certainly not the Czechoslovak Government and no one can pretend they are. So that without any permission or request from the Czechoslovak Government this interference, this invasion did take place."

Lord Caradon of the United Kingdom joined his American colleague, saying that the Council would "have no difficulty at all in choosing between this turgid and apparently

THE CZECHOSLOVAKIAN CRISIS

anonymous document on the one hand, and the authenticated, authoritative, convincing and moving statements which have been made to us this evening by the representative of Czechoslovakia."

At the next meeting of the Security Council, August 22, Lord Caradon again paid tribute to the Czech representative, to his Government "and to all the leaders of his brave country who have refused to bow down before the forces of invasion and suppression."

Ambassador Borch of Denmark then read a draft resolution introduced by him and six other delegations (Brazil, Canada, France, Paraguay, the United States and the United Kingdom). An eighth member, Senegal, joined these seven sponsors later in the day.

> "*The Security Council,*
>
> *Recalling* that the United Nations is based on the principle of the sovereign equality of all its Members,
>
> *Gravely concerned* that, as announced by the Presidium of the Central Committee of the Communist Party in Czechoslovakia, troops of the Soviet Union and other members of the Warsaw Pact have entered their country without the knowledge and against the wishes of the Czechoslovakian Government,
>
> *Considering* that the action taken by the Government of the Union of Soviet Socialist Republics and other members of the Warsaw Pact in invading the Czechoslovak Socialist Republic is a violation of the United Nations Charter and, in particular, of the principle that all Members shall refrain in their international relations from the threat of use of force against the territorial integrity or political indepedence of any State,
>
> *Gravely concerned* also by risks of violence and reprisals as

well as by threats to individual liberty and human rights which cannot fail to result from imposed military occupation,

Considering that the people of the sovereign State of the Czechoslovak Socialist Republic have the right in accordance with the Charter freely to exercise their own self-determination and to arrange their own affairs without external intervention,

1. *Affirms* that the sovereign, political independence and territorial integrity of the Czechoslovak Socialist Republic must be fully respected,

2. *Condemns* the armed intervention of the Union of Soviet Socialist Republics and other members of the Warsaw Pact in the internal affairs of the Czechoslovak Socialist Republic and calls upon them to take no action of violence or reprisal that could result in further suffering or loss of life, forthwith to withdraw their forces, and to cease all other forms of intervention in Czechoslovakia's internal affairs;

3. *Calls upon* Members of States of the United Nations to exercise their diplomatic influence upon the Union of Soviet Socialist Republics and the other countries concerned with a view to bringing about prompt implementation of this resolution;

4. *Requests* the Secretary-General to transmit this resolution to the countries concerned, to keep the situation under constant review, and to report to the Council on compliance with this resolution."

In the discussion which followed the introductory remarks of the representative of Denmark, the sponsors presented their point of view. Ambassador Malik of the Soviet

THE CZECHOSLOVAKIAN CRISIS

Union reserved the right to speak at the next meeting. At the first meeting he merely responded to the statement of the United States representative who had denied that only imperialists had opposed the Soviet intervention in Czechoslovakia and had named the Prime Minister of India, Pope Paul and the Presidents of Romania, Yugoslavia and Tanzania as being among the "imperialist" protesters. Ambassador Malik called the American representative "the main orchestra leader of the repulsive comedy which started yesterday" and repeated his charge that "the participation of imperialism in this whole business is a fact." He corroborated his assertion with a lengthy quotation from a statement just received from the Tass Agency in Moscow according to which the situation in Czechoslovakia had remained normal. "The counter-revolutionaries are using clandestine radio transmitters and printing presses which were prepared beforehand. The slanderous fabrications and inventions cooked up by counter-revolutionaries and transmitted in this way are taken up by imperialist propaganda which is trying to pass them off as an expression of the official position of Czechoslovakia and its public opinion." Ambassador Malik made a great effort to show, on the basis of the Tass statement, "how false, how hypocritical were these crocodile tears shed by the representatives of imperialist Powers to pretend that they were defending socialism in Czechoslovakia." And he concluded:

> "The Security Council has never seen anything more preposterous, more ridiculous, more repulsive, than the sight of representatives of monopoly capital playing the role of defenders of socialism and communism, even defenders of socialist unity. The socialist countries and their peoples loudly proclaim, with full conviction and officially for all to hear,

that the imperialists should not stick their noses into socialist and communist affairs; otherwise they may lose their noses."

Lord Caradon and Ambassador Ball answered him immediately. Caradon objected to calling the proceedings of the Security Council "a repulsive comedy;" rather he said, it was a "repulsive tragedy which is taking place in Czechoslovakia as a result of the evil intervention of the Soviet Union." Lord Caradon also stated that "when we wish to be informed about Czechoslovakia we go to the Czechoslovakians and not to Tass." He recalled that "the Soviet Union has repeated its adherence to the principle of non-interference in the affairs of other States; their intervention has made a mockery of this, particularly coming, as it does, a bare fortnight after their public reaffirmation of that principle in Bratislava." He also expressed his trust in the Security Council:

> "Our duty here in this Council is clear. We should not hesitate to adopt the draft resolution and to adopt it without delay. Some people say that there is no force or effect in resolutions. Not so. It is clearly of the utmost necessity and urgency that the invasion be immediately condemned in the clearest terms. So the Czechoslovak leaders believe, and they are the best judges. That is our immediate duty. We should not fail to do it. We should not fail to do it now."

Ambassador Ball exercised his right of reply to state that he was not defending socialism or communism but freedom in Czechoslovakia. He reminded the Security Council, as Lord Caradon had done, "that the Soviet representative has made no attempt to reply to the utterly damning statements which were made by the leaders of the Czechoslovak Government

THE CZECHOSLOVAKIAN CRISIS

and which were read to us last night by the Acting Permanent Representative of Czechoslovakia." Ball finished his statement by reverting to a custom of his predecessor, Arthur Goldberg, who had been in the habit of interspersing his responses with quotations from literature. The United States Ambassador stressed that the attitude displayed by the Soviet representative toward the reaction of the Czechoslovak people reminded him of an anecdote told by Jonathan Swift. "This dog," Swift had said, "is vicious and dangerous and should be destroyed. When attacked he defends himself."

* * *

A race against time then developed in the Security Council. The President informed the Council that a majority of the delegations had expressed the wish to hold the next meeting at 4 p.m., the same day. Some delegations had preferred 6 p.m.; he proposed a compromise, namely 5 or 5:30 p.m. This simple detail provoked a lengthy discussion.

Ambassador Bouattoura of Algeria proposed to adjourn with no set time for the next meeting, urging that it be convened after consultations had taken place. Ambassador Ball strongly opposed the motion, giving as his reason that "meanwhile the occupation is being consolidated in Czechoslovakia; people are being imprisoned; people are disappearing, the troops are imposing martial law." Ambassador Tardos of Hungary supported his colleague from Algeria. Ambassador Ignatieff of Canada and Lord Caradon of the United Kingdom took the floor to express their preference for 5 p.m. When the President was about to take a vote, Ambassador Malik raised a point of order. "I see no grounds," he said, "for pushing matters to a vote." He had the impression that the

WAR ON WAR

United States representative had "a burning desire to exert pressure on the members and the President of the Council." The President denied that any pressure was being exerted on him and finally put to a vote the motion to adjourn until 5 p.m. This motion was adopted by 10 votes in favor, none opposed and 5 abstentions. By then it was 1:25 p.m.

The next meeting did not begin at 5 p.m. but only at 9 p.m. The representatives of Czechoslovakia, Bulgaria and Poland were invited, at their request, to take seats at the table.

After reading some messages he had received, the representative of Czechoslovakia summarized the situation as follows:

> "First, the occupation of the Czechoslovak Socialist Republic by the Foreign armed forces is completely illegal;
> Second, only the legally elected constitutional representatives are the true representatives of the Czechoslovak Socialist Republic and its people, and consequently must be enabled to exercise freely their constitutional functions, without illegal interference by the occupation forces;
> Third, all the acts of the foreign occupation forces in the Czechoslovak Socialist Republic are illegal;
> Fourth, complete and immediate termination of the occupation, the withdrawal of all occupation forces from the territory of the Czechoslovak Socialist Republic and the full restitution of the sovereignty and territorial integrity of the Czechoslovak Socialist Republic are imperative."

He informed the Council that the Minister for Foreign Affairs of Czechoslovakia was on his way to New York. A discussion ensued, raising a new problem. The representative of Bulgaria asked for the floor in order to get permission to speak "tomorrow instead of today." His stated reason was that

THE CZECHOSLOVAKIAN CRISIS

he wanted to prepare his speech "a little further if possible." The President refused to commit himself because he did not know whether the matter would not "come to a vote today."

Ambassador Malik intervened, expressing his surprise "why we cannot take into account and entertain the request of the representative of Bulgaria and allow him to speak tomorrow." He said that he, too, would prefer to speak on the next day only. "Why should the Council suddenly show such unseemly haste?" the Soviet Ambassador demanded.

The President explained that in calling the meeting, he had acted at the request of ten delegations. The other five delegations had also been consulted. He would have no objection to the representative of Bulgaria speaking on the next day only, but he could not be certain that there would be a meeting at that time at all. Ambassador Malik was not satisfied, however. He interrupted again. "We know that majority," he said, "we have known it ever since the creation of the United Nations and the Security Council." The Soviet Ambassador asked to "apply democratic principles in this case" and to "put an end to this meeting." The President then asked for the comment of the members of the Security Council. Ambassador Ball took the floor:

> "The representative of the Soviet Union does us all a very great disservice because he indicates such a low opinion of our sophistication, of our understanding of what is really happening tonight.
> What we are witnessing is a shameless and shoddy and desperate effort on the part of the representative of the Soviet Union, of the representative of Hungary, of the representative of Bulgaria, to delay and frustrate the proceedings of this Council at a very critical moment in its history."

WAR ON WAR

The American Ambassador expressed his satisfaction that "a brave, decent, honest man came here this evening to explain to the Council, in clear, straightforward and unmistakable terms, the position of his Government, the legitimate Government of Czechoslovakia." He said also that it would be "a privilege for all of us to greet the Foreign Minister of Czechoslovakia, Jiri Hajek, when he comes before this body tomorrow." Concerning the Security Council's position in the entire problem, he said:

> "This is an evening, tonight, in the life of the Security Council when the whole world is making a hard appraisal as to whether this institution, which we have developed and nourished for almost a quarter of a century, is capable of facing up to a major and tragic and dangerous event that has torn the fabric of world confidence and brutally halted progress towards a more secure peace."

As a creation of human beings, Ambassador Ball continued, the Council was subject to the temptation "not merely of corruption from venality" but to the "temptation to falter and to fail from lack of faith in itself and from cynicism in its own high purpose." This was why the advice" to delay, proceed cautiously, await the movement of events" had been given "by the two guilty Governments represented in this body." This was not "a counsel of prudence" but "a counsel of deception, advice given not in goodwill but for an evil purpose." The representatives of the two Powers "whose Governments participated in the rape of Czechoslovakia" are "quite obviously hoping that this body will delay its action, that they can frustrate its action long enough for a new synthetic government to send a message or a representative to this Council to ask the

THE CZECHOSLOVAKIAN CRISIS

Council not to consider the question now before us." Ball called it "a shoddy performance" which carried a message to the Security Council to "measure up to its responsibilities."

> "The brutal assault on Czechoslovakia occurred the night before last and the Security Council, charged with the very special mandate that it has to protect the security of the world and to protect world peace, has not yet spoken. Every effort has been made by the Soviet representative to delay and impede our proceedings by long, meandering, diffuse, polemical and irrelevant statements, and I am sure we will have much more of the same tonight as we already have. In fact, I would not be at all surprised if in the course of this evening the representative of the Soviet Union read to us excerpts from the Moscow telephone directory. And quite likely, if he reads enough of them they will include the names of some who are included in the new Czech Government."

The American Ambassador said further:

> "What we are told with the inimitable elegance and sensitivity of the Soviet representative's phraseology is that if this body should, and I quote him, 'stick its nose into the affairs of the Soviet's Eastern European colonial empire it would lose its nose.' These are harsh, ominous, rude, vulgar words, words recalling earlier and more primitive chapters in the long history of human society, words fraught with menace which I know we have all been shocked to hear in the proceedings of this Council."

Ball then called for a vote on the draft resolution. However, Ambassador Malik immediately raised a point of order:

WAR ON WAR

"Mr. Ball has weak nerves. This is an obvious sign of the fact that American imperialism has failed in playing the card of counter-revolution in Czechoslovakia and that is why Mr. Ball becomes so agitated and cannot hide his condition. In this Security Council he has spoken with such gestures and with such a tone as if he were sitting at a meeting of subordinates in a bank. Mr. Ball, this is not your office here . . .

Mr. Ball, you have no right to prevent those who want to speak from speaking . . . You have often spoken of democracy and freedom; you even took it upon yourself to speak as a so-called defender of socialism. It is true that later, when confronted with concrete facts, you stepped back and admitted that you were not defending socialism and communism. But nobody expected you to do so . . ."

Ambassador Malik referred to the history of the social democratic movement in Germany and quoted Bebel, who had once said in the German *Reichstag:* "Bebel is an old fool. If you are praised by a bourgeois you must have made a mistake." Malik analogized the reference to the Czechoslovak situation: If a communist or socialist is praised by an imperialist (*i.e.*, Ball), a "true patriot" must have made a mistake. He then attacked Ball for "unveiling a rather interesting secret to the Security Council"; namely, the arrival of the Foreign Minister of Czechoslovakia. How did he know that? Had he, perhaps arranged for this visit himself?

The Soviet Ambassador, reverting to the tradition of his predecessor, Fedorenko, quoted a proverb (though not Chinese but Russian): "Some people can talk, but others had better remain silent." After addressing Mr. Ball directly, Ambassador Malik returned to the initial subject of discussion: Why should the representative of Bulgaria not "be afforded the courtesy of being able to speak tomorrow?"

THE CZECHOSLOVAKIAN CRISIS

Ambassador Tarabanov of Bulgaria joined Malik and again asked for permission to speak on the next day. The President again repeated that he would be only too glad to grant such permission if the Council were indeed to meet that day.

Exercising the right of reply, Ambassador Ball corrected the impression that he had been privy to a secret in knowing of the expected arrival of the Czechoslovak Minister for Foreign Affairs. This information, he said, had been supplied by the Acting Permanent Representative of Czechoslovakia, who had previously made an official announcement of the visit.

The Soviet Ambassador returned to the issue of the Bulgarian representative's right to wait until the next day to speak, "after a good night's sleep." Ambassador Ignatieff of Canada again opposed procrastination, whereupon the Soviet Ambassador explained that "the American and the Englishman" were being guilty of procrastination because they had wasted four hours in the afternoon. "If you had not engaged in this procrastination," said Ambassador Malik, "we would all have been in bed now." And he concluded:

> "Let us agree that the representative of Bulgaria will be able to speak in the morning, ten hours from now. Really, nothing extraordinary will happen in those ten hours."

The President was unable to bring the matter to a vote without an interruption by the Soviet Ambassador. When the President advised the Council that he had no speakers on his list but that "two delegations" had "signified their intention of speaking after the vote," the Soviet Ambassador interpreted it as meaning that there was "no intention to afford an opportunity to the representative of Bulgaria to take the floor." The

President corrected this impression by saying that he was ready to give him the floor "right away." When the Canadian Ambassador moved to proceed to the vote on the draft resolution, Mr. Malik again stated that he considered this as "expressing his desire to deprive the representative of Bulgaria of the possibility of speaking." The President again offered to "recognize him at any time, even now." The Bulgarian Ambassador again asked whether it was not possible for him to speak at the next meeting of the Security Council. Finally, Ambassador Ball said:

> "The hour is late, and I must say, speaking for my Government, that I can express a sentiment which I am certain is shared around this table. It is a matter of grave concern to find this solemn body turned into a circus by the most absurd, ridiculous proposals intended to obstruct the exercise by this body of the expression of its opinion, which is long overdue, on a crisis which is confronting the world, which is resulting in the destruction of a legitimate Government, which is threatening the peace of the world. To have us at this point consume hours—literally hours—on this kind of grotesque procedural nonsense is I think an affront to all of us. We are accomplices if we permit this to go on very much further—accomplices in undermining the dignity of the United Nations and the dignity of the Security Council."

Ambassador Malik took the floor again, asking "the representative of the United States to be patient." He then delivered a long speech which takes up over twenty-five pages in the Verbatim Record. It dealt with the American and British attitude towards the events in Czechoslovakia. The Soviet Ambassador asserted that there had been interference in the affairs of Czechoslovakia from outside (from "imperialist cir-

THE CZECHOSLOVAKIAN CRISIS

cles" in the United States, Great Britain, Western Germany and a series of other countries). He described at length what the Soviet Union had done for Czechoslovakia. As to the Czechoslovak Representative's statements in the Council, he commented as follows:

> "Yesterday the Czechoslovak representative stated that he had received statements by radio, but that he was not sure that they were altogether literally correct. Today, he left the hall, having made a very short statement, without saying a word to anyone. This is a rather strange attitude. It would seem that not everything is in order, and much of what he said here was previously published in the United States Press and even by the OPI of the United Nations, which is also a stronghold of the United States."

When Ambassador Malik had ended his speech, the President again asked the representative of Bulgaria whether he wished to address the Council. The response was that the Bulgarian representative wished to speak before the vote would be taken. The President interpreted this to mean that "at this stage" the representative of Bulgaria did not wish to speak, and returned to the Canadian motion. Ambassador Malik again had a point of order:

> "I asked for the floor before. If you call on the representative of Bulgaria. I have no objection."

After that, the President recognized the representative of the United States. Ambassador Malik asserted another point of order, but Ambassador Ball did not yield.

Finally, Ambassador Tarabanov of Bulgaria was given the floor. His point was that in the present circumstances the Security Council and the United Nations had "no business

WAR ON WAR

interfering in the domestic affairs of a socialist country that did not seek help from it." Some further statements were made "in explanation of the vote" and finally the vote on the eight-Power draft resolution was taken. Ten votes were in favor (Brazil, Canada, China, Denmark, Ethiopia, France, Paraguay, Senegal, United Kingdom and United States), two opposed (Hungary and Soviet Union) and three abstentions (Algeria, India, Pakistan). The President then announced that, owing to the negative vote of one permanent member of the Security Council, the draft resolution had failed of adoption.

This, the 105th veto by the Soviet Union, was followed by a number of speeches. The meeting adjourned at 3:55 a.m. on Friday, August 23, 1968. The President announced that the next meeting would be held at 5 p.m. "tomorrow"— meaning, of course, Friday, August 23, 1968.

* * *

While winning the race against time in the Security Council, the eight Powers lost the battle. The veto of the Soviet Union had defeated the draft resolution.

Before the adjournment of the Thursday night meeting, Canada, on behalf of the eight delegations, introduced the following new draft resolution:

"*The Security Council,*

Concerned at reports about the current developments in Czechoslovakia including the arrest of Czechoslovak leaders,

Requests the Secretary-General to appoint and despatch immediately to Prague a Special Representative who shall seek the release and ensure the personal safety of the Czecho-

THE CZECHOSLOVAKIAN CRISIS

slovak leaders under detention and who shall report back urgently."

This draft resolution, immediately condemned by Ambassador Malik as "a new trick of the NATO countries in this dirty, shoddy business," was before the Security Council when it was convened at 5 p.m. on August 23.

Ambassador Malik again opposed the inclusion of the Canadian draft resolution in the agenda, calling it "an open, direct and cynical attempt to impose on the Council the customary imperialist practice which consists of using the United Nations in order to achieve their hidden objectives." The Soviet Ambassador stressed that "having failed in their designs in the Security Council, the representatives of the Western Powers are resorting to a new act of provocation with the same goal in view." There was "not the slightest doubt," he said, that this was "an activity contrary to the cause of peace and security of peoples." Behind the back of the representative of Canada one could "see the looming shadow of the representative of the United States, of course, and further the more attenuated shadow of the representative of Britain." To explain the meaning of the new draft resolution, Ambassador Malik used a Russian proverb: "Take the same soup, although it is somewhat thinner." He stated clearly that "the Soviet delegation, upon instruction of the Soviet Government, has several times stated in this Council that the Soviet Union considered that the discussion on the question inscribed on the agenda and imposed on the Security Council is groundless and contrary to the Charter." However, when the President announced that he was going to take a vote on the adoption of the agenda, Malik opposed and asked:

WAR ON WAR

> "But has anybody suggested that the matter be settled by a vote?"

Ambassador Ball reacted immediately:

> I see no reason why we should play the same bad comedy every other night. We had this problem before us, I think, two nights ago. The Soviet Union objected to the inscription of certain items on the agenda, and then, when it came to the question whether the Council should express its will on the inscription of those items, the Soviet Union took the position that it did not want to vote."

His reference to the Soviet intervention as "a bad comedy" drew the following answer from Ambassador Malik:

> "During the debate on the question imposed on the Council by the delegation of the United States and Britain, we were able many times to convince ourselves that the most ludicrous comedies were those played out here by the representative of the United States; he was the main comedian here. So that is that, as far as comedies are concerned."

In the substance of the matter, Malik again insisted that he did not ask for a vote. The American representative, he said, "has an inordinate fondness for votes. He just loves votes. 'Vote, vote, vote. Vote. Hurry up, vote.' We have seen that at our previous night meeting." Ambassador Malik felt that "if there is no proposal that the question not be inscribed on the agenda, there is no reason to vote."

Ambassador Ball agreed, in his next response, that he did have "a great fondness for votes." He explained this love for votes as follows:

THE CZECHOSLOVAKIAN CRISIS

"We have a democratic tradition in this country, and I can well understand the allergy which my Soviet colleague feels for the resort to the democratic process."

The procedural quarrel was finally settled by the President's statement that since he had heard no objections, he would take it that the agenda had been adopted. No vote was taken, the agenda was adopted and discussion of the merits of the issue began.

Ambassador Ignatieff of Canada, the first to speak, called the new draft resolution a "straightforward, uncomplicated, humanitarian proposal." He would not, he said, follow the representative of the Soviet Union "in an exchange of incivilities and accusations". The proposal put forward in the name of eight delegations was seeking to get some assurance about the treatment of acknowledged leaders of Czechoslovakia. So far as the issue was concerned, it "has been, and continues to be, the inadmissibility under the Charter of intervention in the internal affairs of any State by any other State."

The French and Danish representatives supported the draft resolution, stressing its humanitarian aspect. In a point of order, the Hungarian representative proposed that the new draft resolution be transferred to other councils and bodies dealing with humanitarian questions. Ambassador Ball stated that the American Government "whole-heartedly" supported the resolution. He referred to Russian history and literature. "It is significant that in the rich and brilliant tradition of the Russian novel, which the whole world reveres and respects, there is a strong tradition of realism," said Ball, "but I found a quite different theme in what the Soviet representative had to say last night." He proceeded to elaborate on his point:

WAR ON WAR

"It is a theme not of realism but of fantasy, for he conjured up two principal fantasy figures. First was the imperialist, an obsessive figure who stalks through the prose of the Soviet representative monotonously, rearing his head every sentence or two. What is this strange shadow figure? As far as I have been able to perceive, an imperialist, quite clearly, is anyone the Soviet Union does not like—anyone with a mind of his own, anyone with a will of his own. There is also a second fantasy figure—the counter-revolutionary. Now, who is the counter-revolutionary? Well, quite obviously he is anyone who gets in the way of the Soviet Union's aggressive designs."

This statement drew an immediate reply from the Soviet representative:

"Mr. Ball tried to tell us that imperialism was anything which the Soviet Union did not like. Well, that is going too far. Mr. Ball has really gone too far this time. Mr. Ball, I think you have in this country all sorts of public opinion polls—Gallup, Harris and others. Why do you not carry out a poll? Ask a question not only among your own citizens but among all those present here: 'Who likes imperialism?' It is a very simple question—three words. Do you really believe that only the representative of the Soviet Union will give a negative answer? I am deeply convinced, Mr. Ball, you representative of large monopoly capital in the United States, that a negative answer will be given by the representatives of Algeria and Burma, the representatives of all Arab countries, and the whole world. The whole world condemns imperialism and its bloody deeds, over many, many years and decades."

Lord Caradon of the United Kingdom appealed to the

THE CZECHOSLOVAKIAN CRISIS

Soviet representative to give some assurance that the President and the First Secretary of the Communist Party and other acknowledged leaders of Czechoslovakia would not be arrested or molested. He mentioned that he had made the same request at the previous meeting of the Security Council and that a "yes" from Ambassador Malik would have been sufficient to make "all of us content." However, the representative of the Soviet Union did not say anything further at the meeting of August 23. Lord Caradon was followed by a representative of Yugoslavia, who was permitted to participate in the debate although his country was not a member of the Security Council. He read a statement of his Government of August 22, expressing "its grave concern over the illegal entry of the armed forces of the Soviet Union and the other four countries into the Czechoslovak Socialist Republic" and condemning the occupation of Czechoslovakia. Yugoslavia felt that "the armed intervention by the aforementioned countries, which has taken place without invitation and against the will of the Government and other constitutional organs of the Czechoslovak Socialist Republic, constitutes a gross violation of the sovereignty and territorial integrity of an independent country, as well as a direct denial of generally recognized principles of international law and the Charter of the United Nations."

The Yugoslav representative, after having read the lengthy statement of his Government, elaborated on it in unmistakable terms. He declared that "Yugoslavia . . . opposes the intervention and occupation of the Czechoslovak Socialist Republic and requests the immediate withdrawal of all occupation troops from the territory of the Czechoslovak Socialist Republic."

The meeting was then adjourned until the next day.

When the Security Council was reconvened on August

24 a new procedural matter came up. The Minister for Foreign Affairs of the German Democratic Republic (East Germany) had sent a telegram to the President of the Security Council requesting that his Government be permitted to participate in the discussion through an authorized representative. The President had sent a photostat of the cable to all members of the Security Council. However, it was not distributed as an official document of the Security Council.

Ambassador Malik read the telegram to the Council and said that "it is more than logical to hear the representative of the German Democratic Republic and authorize him to take part in the debate." He also felt that "it goes without saying that [the telegram] must be published as an official document of the Security Council."

The representatives of France and the United Kingdom did not agree. Their governments did not recognize East Germany, and they expressed an opinion that "to hear the person who asked to be heard would add nothing new . . . would only serve to delay and confuse the proceedings, which indeed doubtless is the object of the application."

Ambassador Ball stated that this was also the view of the United States Government. He added some comment in order "to examine why this problem has come before us."

> "To anyone who had the great misfortune to have to endure the filibuster by the Soviet representative Thursday night, the primary purpose of this latest Soviet manoeuvre will be all too clear. That purpose is to provide an issue in the Council which may, for a moment at least, distract our attention from the development of events in Czechoslovakia. While it is true that the regime established by the Soviet Union in the zone of Germany which it has occupied since the close of

THE CZECHOSLOVAKIAN CRISIS

the Second World War is an accomplice in the crime now before the Council, Ambassador Malik is under no illusions about the usefulness to him or even the novelty of testimony before the Council from still another of the occupiers of Czechoslovakia.

The request which is now before us from the Soviet representative has therefore a quality of effrontery. What is shocking in the extreme is that the Czechoslovakian peoples, who suffered the brutal occupation of their country by Hitler's armies in 1938, should again have been subjected to the indignity of invasion and occupation by German troops, this time under despotic leaders sponsored and kept in power by the Soviet Union.

All we could expect from listening to a representative of the so-called German Democratic Republic would be a lengthening of that long chain of incoherencies, irrelevancies and redundancies with which we have already been presented by the Soviet Union and its client States."

Ambassador Borch of Denmark joined his colleagues from France, the United Kingdom and the United States in opposing the request by East Germany. He added only "that we should let no doubt arise that the action of invasion by itself can be no passport to this Council."

Ambassador Malik again advocated approval of East Germany's request. In a speech taking up ten pages of the Verbatim Record he defended the right of any State "to unmask at meetings of the Security Council hostile statements, innuendos, insinuations, misrepresentations, fabrications of the representatives of the imperialist bloc." He was particularly sensitive to the term "filibuster" used by Ambassador Ball in reference to the Soviet representative's tactics:

WAR ON WAR

"Mr. Ball mentioned the well-known term 'filibuster.' In Russian that word does not exist. The thing does not exist. Russians never engage in filibusters. It is an Anglo-Saxon practice, I will have you know. Lord Caradon seems to nod in agreement. Therefore, please, do not tell us that we are doing something that is entirely yours.

What was going on in previous meetings? A meeting of the Council had been called for 5 o'clock. But then our Anglo-Saxon filibusterers had the meeting postponed until 9 o'clock. What has that to do with us, I ask you? The debates were protracted. We had to meet at night. And that is why the United States representative nervously kept asking for a vote. He wanted to go to bed. So, Sir, if you want to speak of filibuster, please speak to yourself. It has nothing to do with us."

Ambassador Malik quoted the Provisional Rules of Procedure of the Council which provided, in Art. 14, that States not members of the United Nations could be invited to participate in a meeting of the Security Council.

The procedural struggle then continued at some length. It also involved the representative of Bulgaria, similarly not a member of the Council, who had been invited to participate in the meeting and now wished to speak. Ambassador Malik delivered another speech taking up fifteen pages of the Verbatim Record, with quotations from German newspapers such as the *Sudeten-Deutsche Zeitung, Frankfurter Allgemeine Zeitung, Nuernberger Nachrichten, Deutsche Nationalzeitung,* to expose the imperialist policy of West Germany. The President made several attempts to solve the procedural tangle caused by the application of East Germany and the distribution of the document. When it finally became clear that nobody had any formal proposal in this matter, Ambassador Malik formulated

THE CZECHOSLOVAKIAN CRISIS

a proposal to invite the representative of the German Democratic Republic to participate in the discussion of the problem on the agenda. A vote was taken. Hungary and the Soviet Union voted for the proposal, nine members were opposed, and four (Algeria, Brazil, India, Pakistan) abstained. The proposal was rejected.

The floor was then given to the Czechoslovak Minister for Foreign Affairs, Jiri Hajek, who had arrived from Europe. "It is not the fault of the Government of the Czechoslovak Socialist Republic that its relations with some other socialist countries have become a matter before the Security Council," said Minister Hajek. He placed the blame on the Governments who had occupied the territory of Czechoslovakia during the night on August 20 and in the morning hours of August 21. "This act of use of force cannot be justified by anything," Hajek stated. "It did not take place upon request or demand of the Czechoslovak Government nor of any other constitutional organs of this Republic." He denied that any request had been made by constitutional political representatives of Czechoslovakia for the country's occupation. "To the knowledge of the Czechoslovak Government no such demand was ever made." The Minister described life in Czechoslovakia prior to the occupation. The Government had been in full control of the country and life was being conducted on a socialist order. The statement, taking up 11 pages of the Verbatim Record, ended with a demand "that the foreign troops—foreign even if they come from friendly countries—leave our country without delay and that the sovereignty of our country may be fully restored and applied throughout its whole territory."

The meeting ended with Ambassador Malik's reading of a Tass telegram from Moscow referring to talks held in the

WAR ON WAR

Kremlin between a delegation from Czechoslovakia headed by President Ludvik Svoboda and the leaders of the Communist Party of the Soviet Union and the Soviet Government. He also read an appeal issued to the citizens of Czechoslovakia by the Governments of the five countries which had occupied Czechoslovakia. Addressed to "our brothers, Czechs and Slovaks," the appeal spoke about the instructions given to "our armed forces to give the working class and the entire Czechoslovak people the necessary help in defence of their socialist gains, which are being threatened with ever more insistent encroachments of internal and international reaction." Ambassador Malik asked that this lengthy appeal be distributed as a document of the Security Council. There being no objection, the President ordered the Secretariat to take the necessary steps to have the document distributed. He then adjourned the meeting with the understanding that the Council would reconvene on Monday, August 26, 1968.

However, this date was not kept. The Security Council never again met on the Czechoslovak crisis. On August 27, 1968, the Acting Permanent Representative of Czechoslovakia, Jan Muzik, addressed the following letter to the President of the Security Council:

> "The agenda of the Security Council includes the item concerning the letter dated 21 August 1968 from the representatives of Canada, Denmark, France, Paraguay, the United Kingdom and the United States to the President of the Security Council (S/8785). I would like to draw your attention to the fact that the Czechoslovak Socialist Republic did not request the inclusion of this item in the agenda of the Security Council. In view of the agreement which has been reached on

THE CZECHOSLOVAKIAN CRISIS

the substance of the problem during Soviet-Czechoslovak talks held in Moscow from 25 August to 26 August 1968, I request you to arrange for the withdrawal of this item from the agenda of the Security Council."

Thus, the Czechoslovak problem was solved for the Security Council.

CHAPTER SEVEN

A POSSIBLE SOLUTION

THE REPORT which the United States delegation of the San Francisco Conference of 1945 submitted to President Harry S. Truman contained the following assertion:

> "If any single provision of the Charter has more substance than the others, it is surely the first sentence of Article 39, which places upon the Security Council the duty to determine the existence of 'any threat to the peace, breach of the peace or act of aggression' and to make recommendations or decide upon measures to be taken 'to maintain or restore international peace and security."

Does this statement hold true today? There is substantial reason to conclude that it does not.

On four occasions that followed one another in brief intervals—in 1950, 1956, 1966 and 1967—the Security Council could do nothing to bring peace to Korea, Vietnam and the Middle East. Twice in 1968, the Security Council failed to solve an international crisis (the "Pueblo Incident" and Czechoslovakia).

In 1950, the Security Council managed to arrive at a decision because one of its permanent members, the Soviet

A POSSIBLE SOLUTION

Union, did not participate in the deliberations. The absent member promptly called the decision illegal, and upon its return, in August 1950, made any further decision impossible by its veto. In 1956, two permanent members, France and the United Kingdom, prevented the Council from reaching a decision. It was only the unusual coalition of two other permanent members, the United States and the Soviet Union, that halted the hostilities in the Middle East that year. In 1966, the Security Council's inability to reach a decision permitted the war in Vietnam to develop into a major disaster. In 1967, the second Middle Eastern war posed a continuing danger for Israel, Jordan, the United Arab Republic and Syria, because the Security Council was in no position to exert the slightest influence on the parties and induce them even to talk to each other.

It is not the veto of a permanent member of the Council that can be blamed for the fiasco of the Security Council. Under present circumstances, different results could not be expected even if there were no provision in Article 27 of the Charter requiring that "decisions of the Security Council . . . shall be made by an affirmative vote of nine members including the concurring votes of the permanent members." This is proved by the fact that two emergency sessions of the General Assembly—where there is no veto power—in 1956 and 1967 produced no better results with regard to the preservation of peace in the Middle East. It is the character of the United Nations organization, rather than its procedure, that makes its peace-making endeavors impotent.

Undoubtedly, the United Nations is a political organization. It is an association of sovereign nations which are jealously protective of their own rights. All insist on having an equal vote, and problems must be resolved by a majority vote.

WAR ON WAR

In terms of world influence, however, can the vote of a country with 200 million inhabitants be equal to the vote of a nation which represents less than one percent of this figure? On the other hand, population is not an adequate measure of influence and there is not, in any event, any real chance of weighing votes on a population basis. Such a reform of the voting system in the Security Council and the General Assembly could never be adopted.

The role presently played by the Security Council in international conflicts is really no different from an exchange of views in the press. The representatives of the nations engage in a debate, sometimes heated, occasionally enlivened by erudite references to Oriental texts or Occidental classics. Never do the arguments rise to the level where they may persuade the "other side." The result is, of course, unproductive.

The repetition of this procedure has caused severe criticism of the role of the United Nations in the preservation of peace. Everyone knows in advance what the representatives of each of the governments will say and how they will vote. No function is served by the open debate.

One solution which could save the United Nations and preserve peace between parties engaged in a conflict would be to submit international differences to impartial arbitration. If such an impartial body could be established which would solve the differences leading to war, or which would establish principles under which war could be stopped, the impasse in which the world finds itself at the present moment might disappear.

Even great powers would find it useful to resort to an impartial body for an evaluation in case of a conflict. The calamity of war and the uncertainty of its outcome makes it preferable to submit to arbitration than to continue with hos-

A POSSIBLE SOLUTION

tilities. The term "honorable peace" might become much more practical if there were a body to which every nation could look with unreserved confidence for an opinion on existing differences. Regardless of whether its provisions corresponded to the wishes of the governments involved in the conflict, the peace worked out by such an impartial body would be an "honorable" one.

An international agency whose function it is to arbitrate issues threatening the peace cannot be a political one. It cannot represent governments. It must have moral authority which would overcome the reservations of the belligerent parties. Sovereign nations will never bow before the verdict of bodies representing other governments; their political prestige would not permit that. In order to overcome the resistance of a belligerent nation, the highest moral authority must be invoked.

Such a moral authority could be created by uniting three factors: (1) the authority of law; (2) the moral force of religion; and (3) the great prestige of individuals who have devoted their lives to the promotion of peace.

The authority of law may be represented by those who either teach law or apply it at the highest level. Religion may be represented by those who are ordained to the ministry and have attained high positions in an ecclesiastical hierarchy. The third group should consist of men with a record of accomplishment for peace—in writing or in practical achievements. The Nobel Foundation pays tribute to such internationally recognized individuals each year.

An agency called upon to arbitrate among belligerent nations should, therefore, be composed of great scholars in jurisprudence (professors of law at universities or supreme court justices), highly-placed representatives of the world's recognized religions, and individuals who have received the Nobel Peace Prize. The members of this body, which should be called "High Commission for Peace," should not hold any positions in the government of the countries of which they are citizens.

This Commission should be headed by a "High Commissioner for Peace," who should be elected by the General Assembly of the United Nations. Once he is elected, it would be his obligation to prepare a suggested list of fifteen members of the High Commission, equally divided among the three groups—law, religion and individual peacemakers. The list should be confirmed by the General Assembly of the United Nations. In addition to the High Commissioner, the Assembly should elect a Deputy Commissioner. Quite obviously, the two principal international political trends—East and West—would be represented in the leadership of the High Commission for Peace. No two members of the Commission should be nationals of the same state.

The High Commission for Peace should be convened within a short time, possibly not later than three days, after the Secretary-General has notified the High Commissioner that the Security Council, by a majority of votes, has confirmed the existence of international hostilities in a given area. The normal activities of the Security Council could proceed until such time as it would become evident that the Security Council was powerless to act because the concurring votes of the permanent members of the Council could not be secured. At that point, the Security Council would merely confirm, by a simple majority vote, the fact that hostilities exist in a certain area. Thereafter, the High Commission for Peace would take over.

The High Commission would issue a demand to the nations involved to cease the hostilities immediately.

A POSSIBLE SOLUTION

The compliance of the belligerents with the demands of the High Commission would be secured by the following procedure: Upon notification by the Secretary-General that a belligerent nation had refused to cease hostilities, the High Commission would, by a majority vote, issue a call to the members of the United Nations to sever trade and economic relations with that nation, and to label it an aggressor. Such a call could also include a demand to all nations to sever diplomatic relations with the aggressor.

Undoubtedly, the moral power of the decision of the High Commission for Peace would be superior to any use of armed force, such as the action by air, sea or land forces provided for in Article 42 of the Charter (which seems to be impractical in any event).

In order to prevent infiltration (including guerilla activities) of the territory of one belligerent by the armed forces of the other, the High Commission could order the border lines controlled by neutral observers.

The final arbitration of the conflict should come by a decision of the High Commission for Peace within a period of six months. This decision should be based on a full investigation of the causes of the conflict and on reports of neutral observers, which would remain secret until such time when they would be released by the High Commission.

If any party to an international conflict should refuse to accept the decision of the High Commission on a permanent settlement of the conflict, sanctions would be applied. The sanctions would consist of the severance of diplomatic, trade and economic relations by all members of the United Nations.

There is little doubt that no nation would risk exclusion from the community of nations by resisting the arbitration decision. Even if it were to do so initially one might expect that after some time it would yield. In that case, the High Commission for Peace would confirm the fact of compliance with its previous decision, and the sanctions would thereupon be revoked.

The provisions on the High Commission for Peace should be made part of the United Nations Chapter. They could be inserted before Chapter VIII, following Article 51 of the present Charter. A tentative draft follows:

The United Nations High Commission for Peace.

Article 52

1. The General Assembly shall, by an absolute majority of all nations voting, elect a High Commissioner for Peace and a Deputy Commissioner for Peace to serve for a term of five years.

2. Nominations of candidates for the offices of High Commissioner and Deputy Commissioner may be made by any permanent member of the Security Council or by agreement of any ten other members of the General Assembly.

3. The High Commissioner and the Deputy Commissioner shall not be nationals of the same state.

4. Neither the High Commissioner nor the Deputy Commissioner shall occupy any governmental office in any member nation during his tenure.

Article 53

1. The High Commissioner shall, within one month after his election, submit to the General Assembly a list of names of

A POSSIBLE SOLUTION

fifteen individuals, no two of whom shall be nationals of the same state, as proposed members of the High Commission for Peace.

2. Five names on the list shall represent the legal profession, either justices of the supreme court in their countries or professors of law at a university; five shall be representatives of religious faiths, and five shall be chosen from among persons who have received the Nobel Peace Prize.

3. The General Assembly shall confirm the members of the High Commission for Peace by simple majority vote.

4. The High Commission for Peace shall consist of the High Commissioner, the Deputy Commissioner, and the fifteen members confirmed as above. In case of the death or incapacity of the High Commissioner, the Deputy Commissioner shall assume the powers and duties of the High Commissioner. He shall, within three months after assuming such powers and duties, appoint, with the consent of a majority of the voting members of the General Assembly, one of the members of the High Commission to serve as Deputy Commissioner.

Article 54

1. The seat of the High Commission shall be at the Headquarters of the United Nations.

2. The Commission shall be authorized to select and appoint a staff pursuant to such terms and conditions as the General Assembly shall, by regulation, establish.

3. The salaries, allowances and compensation of the members of the High Commission for Peace shall be borne by

the United Nations in such manner as the General Assembly shall determine.

4. The members of the High Commission for Peace shall enjoy all diplomatic privileges and immunities.

Article 55

1. The High Commissioner for Peace shall convene the Commission within three days of the submission to him by the Secretary-General of a notification that the Security Council by a majority of votes, has confirmed that international hostilities have broken out in a given area. The provision of Article 27, Par. 3. of the Charter concerning the necessity of concurring votes of the permanent members of the Council does not apply to this decision of the Security Council.

2. The Commission is empowered to issue, by a majority vote, a demand to the nations involved to cease hostilities immediately.

Article 56

1. If the Secretary-General notifies the High Commissioner for Peace that any belligerent nation has refused to cease hostilities, the High Commission for Peace shall immediately establish that this nation has committed an act of aggression. The High Commission, by a majority vote, shall call upon the members of the United Nations to sever trade and economic relations with the aggressor nation. It may also include a call to sever diplomatic relations with the aggressor.

2. If it finds it necessary, the High Commission for Peace shall order, by a majority vote, that the borders which existed prior to the start of hostilities shall be under control of neutral

A POSSIBLE SOLUTION

observers in order to prevent infiltration of the territory of one belligerent by the armed forces of the other.

Article 57

1. The High Commission for Peace shall, within a period of six months, after the notification by the Secretary-General in accordance with Article 55, decide, by a majority vote of its members, on a permanent arbitration of the conflict which caused the outbreak of the hostilities.

2. Before deciding on a settlement, the Commission shall conduct a full investigation into the causes of the conflict.

3. The High Commission is empowered to direct states which are not alleged to be involved in the hostilities to send observers to the area of the conflict. The reports of the observers to the High Commission shall remain secret until the High Commission decides to release them.

Article 58

1. If any party to an international conflict refuses to accept the decision of the High Commission for Peace on a permanent settlement of the conflict, the High Commission shall issue a call to all members of the United Nations to sever diplomatic, trade and economic relations with such nation.

2. Such sanctions shall continue in effect until the nation which refused to accept the High Commission's settlement complies with this settlement and the High Commission confirms, by a majority vote, the fact of such compliance.

(*Present Article 52 of the United Nations Charter would follow as Article 59, etc.*)

Augsburg College
George Sverdrup Library
Minneapolis, Minnesota 55404